Wingwalking

A MEMOIR

by

Steven Slater

Wingwalking: A Memoir
by: Steven Slater

Original Publication: February 24, 2020
Printed in The United States of America Copyright

PUBLISHER:
On It Media, LLC.
107 S West Street, #136
Alexandria, VA 22314
www.onit.tv

*To my angels, seen and unseen,
in the City of Angels and beyond.*

Table of Contents

Table of Contents..5

INTRODUCTION...7

CHAPTER 1...12

CHAPTER 2...25

CHAPTER 3...36

CHAPTER 4...47

CHAPTER 5...55

CHAPTER 6...68

CHAPTER 7...82

CHAPTER 8...94

CHAPTER 9...103

CHAPTER 10...120

CHAPTER 11...129

CHAPTER 12...146

CHAPTER 13...157

CHAPTER 14...172

CHAPTER 15...183

CHAPTER 16...195

CHAPTER 17...202

CHAPTER 18...210

INTRODUCTION

S hadows grew long in the hazy summer air, suffocating the city. I laid broken in a debris-strewn alley off Skid Row. Radiant heat pulsated from the pavement as I took refuge between two hulking dumpsters spilling over with billowing, black garbage bags. Frenzied rats scurried unabashedly about the alley as I laid upon urine-stained weather-beaten cardboard, shielded from discarded hypodermic needles and inky grime that clung to my damp palms and smudged my fevered face. My backpack, heavily laden with my few remaining belongings, had worn my shoulders raw and a thin trickle of deep, red blood seeped through my t-shirt above my right collarbone. I was parched and desperate for food and water but had lost my wallet in the crescendo of panic that sent me scrambling to the street in flight from the voices and their sardonic and diabolic threats. And now, I could run no farther. Propped up against the grungy brick wall hiding from the prying eyes of the world above, I surveyed my desolate and desperate situation. And conceded defeat.

I rolled onto my back and looked up into the grey sky above. In a moment, the sound of jet engines filled the airspace above. I watched the pristine, white aircraft float slowly and elegantly overhead then bank toward the airport. Suddenly, I was struck by a crushing sadness as I watched the majestic liner grow smaller in the distance, leaving me behind, alone in the squalor. A few minutes passed as I lay reeling in the shadows reflecting on the staggering losses that shattered my heart and drove me from my mind and into the filthy alley—in much the same manner a wounded animal would while slinking away in search of privacy in the last vestiges of life. With each passing airliner I watched descend into the setting sun, I became more acutely aware of how profoundly I had been utterly discarded by a world that had no further need of me. I thought of my son, now lost to me. I began to mourn for my mother who had died a few years earlier as my heart broke anew.

The rumble of approaching jet engines filled the alley again, breaking the reverie. Suddenly, I was enveloped by the shadow of a massive 777 passing low and slow. She was breathtaking as she banked, her nose lifted regally in the California sun, with her "Delta" titles easily readable down the fuselage. My heart lurched as I remembered floating down the aisle of this very aircraft high over the Atlantic each week making witty, casual conversation with my cosmopolitan passengers. I wondered who her crew was, knowing a few of us had probably toasted life at Ferdinand's in Paris or danced beneath the stars on the teak deck of the Patricia in Stockholm Harbor. Could they now see me cowering in the rancid alley below?

As the sleek and shiny Boeing slipped further away, I reached my hand out to it as a single tear fell from my eye. Soon the jetliner disappeared on the horizon, leaving me gutted in the twilight. Here remained nothing of the winsome, privileged life of travel and romance I had so cherished.

I turned my head from the sky as something shiny caught my eye. Green and jagged, the broken glass shards loomed a few inches from my face. I regarded them vacantly for a moment, then seemingly without thought, I picked up a sharp piece between my thumb and forefinger. I held the shard up to the last light of day and noted the glint of sun off its rough but sharp, translucent edges. In that moment, I recognized the inevitability of what I was about to do.

I was crushed by an aching sadness the magnitude of which I had never known before. Suddenly, I understood that I had crept into that alley to die. Alone, in obscurity, I would leave the earth. I was a newsmaker and a pop culture icon. I had done countless television interviews and appeared in glossy magazine spreads. And now, I would die in desolation with no identification. I found that achingly tragic. My eyes welled with tears and I let out a racking, short sob as the irony of the moment hit me with resounding clarity.

I held up my right arm and began to regard the well-pronounced veins in my wrist. I brought the glass gently against the soft flesh as I prepared to make the cut. I paused for a second and looked at the shattered glass in my hand, then I looked around at the grimy alley and at the gritty, crumbling brick buildings on either side of me. At the rats and the litter and the grime. And suddenly, I was jarringly and resoundingly revolted by the whole affair. Seemingly from some until-then unheard place deep within, I grew intensely offended and profoundly affronted.

"NO!" I yelled out firmly. "THIS...is NOT where this ends!" In that moment, I threw aside the unrelenting sadness of my staggering grief and took up rage and indignation in its place.

I carefully placed the shard of glass beneath one of the dumpsters and staggered to my feet.

"FUCK YOU!" I screamed up to the sky, my fists clenched at my sides. "FUCKING DO SOMETHING, NOW!" I railed at my Higher Power, standing amidst the shattered glass, rotting garbage, and the discarded syringes, shaking with rage, hot tears stinging my face.

Suddenly, I lurched towards the street, my heavy backpack slung over my bloodied shoulder.

It was dark now and the city streets were deserted. I was quickly whipping myself up into a state of hysteria and crossing into bipolar mania. My heart threatened to burst from my chest as adrenaline coursed wildly through my veins. I was enraged now, terrified of my own anger. Making matters worse, I was now lost in the depths of the dark city. I was overwhelmed by both the frightening and unfamiliar sights and sounds of downtown but also the intense emotional firestorm consuming my psyche and driving me further into danger.

I began obsessing on the piece of glass hidden safely beneath the dumpster, knowing I could use it and bring this nightmare to an efficient and resounding end once and for all. "HOSPITAL! I NEED A FUCKING HOSPITAL!" I wailed as I stormed urgently up 6th Street in disoriented terror.

"DON'T LEAVE ME OUT HERE TO DIE LIKE A FUCKING ANIMAL, YOU SON OF A BITCH!" I yelled out hoarsely at God across the empty night street. And then, in a miracle of biblical proportions, the Red Line station appeared ahead like a mirage and soon I was sitting on the train, crying softly, and racing beneath the city at a dizzying speed toward Hollywood and the one hospital I knew.

I felt like I was swimming underwater when I stumbled through the sliding doors at Kaiser Sunset and up to the desk in the emergency room. A pleasant and poised young receptionist smiled sweetly and asked me how she could help. I stood baffled in front of the desk unable to speak, overwhelmed with embarrassment, sorrow, and shame. "I...I...want to die," I said haltingly, choking back tears.

The receptionist's green eyes were warm with understanding as she tilted her head to the side slightly. "I'm so sorry. It's so hard sometimes, isn't it?" she asked and reached for my hand across the counter. She quickly looked across the lobby and made eye contact with a virile and stern-looking Latino security guard in a sharp, gray uniform. With a barely perceptible nod, she motioned him over. Speaking softly, she asked my name and a little more about how I came to arrive at the hospital. I said I was bipolar and had gotten lost downtown. I said I was tired and that I couldn't do it anymore. By now the guard was standing with us and momentarily, we were joined by an upbeat, male nurse who smiled brightly and introduced himself. He was a reassuring presence and I began to feel a little safer and more relaxed. He asked me to repeat what I said to the others and to tell him about the last 24 hours in detail. I told him about being overwhelmed and weary and so angry. I repeated that I did not want to live anymore. He nodded understandingly.

"Steven," he said gently but directly holding my gaze, "do you want to kill yourself tonight?" I nodded, tears welling up in my eyes. "Okay," he replied steadily, then asked, "Do you have a plan for how you will kill yourself tonight?"

I paused, swimming through my embarrassment and shame, then said slowly and deliberately, "There is an alley downtown, and I have hidden a piece of broken glass under a dumpster there. I am going back there to open a vein and bleed out." I lifted my right arm and pointed to my wrist.

At once, the crushing sadness from the alley descended upon me again and I began to wail with racking sobs. I gasped for air as the room went dark. My knees gave out and suddenly I was falling backwards and down to the floor. And then at once, I was lifted up into the strong and steady arms of the beautiful guard who carried me like a frightened child across the lobby and into the brightly lit triage room as I cried with relief into his broad and solid chest.

"It's okay, my friend. We got this," the guard whispered down to me with a sly smile and a wink as he set me down on a stretcher like a rag doll. And within minutes, I fell fast asleep in the City of Angels.

CHAPTER 1

I made my debut on December 6th, 1971, in Long Beach, California, to my mother Diane, a former runway model and stewardess and my father David, an American Airlines pilot. I bear an angry scar on my lower abdomen from the emergency surgery that took place when it was discovered that I was born without a urethra, a condition known as hypospadias, a little-known but life-threatening condition which affects 1 in every 200 children. I was pulled from my mother's arms and whisked into surgery where a catheter was bored directly through my gut and into my bladder, the first of a long and excruciating series of reconstructive surgeries that left both my body and psyche riddled with scars I have long sought peace with.

At two weeks, I was taken to Children's Hospital in Hollywood where an artificial urethra was crafted by surgical incision and by using a series of rods to stretch open the newly-minted passageway. While I blessedly don't recall the first barbaric procedures, the natural growth and development of my body meant repeating parts of the appalling sequence each year until age fourteen.

I lived in terror of the annual checkup where I was handed over to a team of masked strangers who laid me, in a flimsy hospital gown, on a freezing cold examination table and violated me in a most humiliating and painful way. The gown was lifted up and I laid embarrassed and exposed and was catheterized, then pumped full of barium dye. The rough and inflexible plastic tubing scraping against the contours of my tender, young insides was excruciating and tears streamed down my cheeks as I bit my tongue to keep from crying out. In my younger years, I was restrained to the table to keep me from jerking or pulling the catheter out. I felt the fullness in my abdomen as it began to rise and bloat. Soon, it would become painful and my panic rose as well. Ultimately, I would become unable to restrain myself any longer and a torrent of dye, urine, and blood would splash across my naked body. I would howl in pain as the catheter slipped from my penis and flailed across the table before slithering to the floor. At that exact moment, a series of X-rays were taken to ensure that my urinary tract was flowing at full capacity with no blockages.

I experienced being restrained, physically violated, and humiliated by a room full of strangers taking pictures as nothing short of torture and rape. A child is unable to comprehend the medical necessity for such torturous procedures. All I knew was that my parents, the very people who were supposed to protect and care for me, handed me over to a room filled with ghostly figures intent on inflicting the worst pain I had ever known. To add an element of confusion to the whole affair, I was simultaneously earning high praise for my ability to withstand this unspeakable abuse and pain. The more of this I took, the greater the praise I earned. These folks, both family and well-intended medical practitioners, were all perfectly lovely people aside from the fact that they tortured me within an inch of my emotional threshold each year. This was all exceptionally overwhelming and confusing to me. For a sex-obsessed, teenage boy suffering intense shame over an emerging "sinful" sexual orientation, it was a source of great shame. When a nocturnal erection caused several stitches in the head of my penis to tear open at the age of thirteen, I believed it was God's punishment for sleeping with older men in the neighborhood.

As a child, I felt responsible for my parents' experience of this whole affair. I saw the revulsion in my father's eyes when he turned away, unable to stomach the sight of the stitches and the wreckage each surgery wrought on my young body when I most needed his comfort and steadfast presence. I felt responsible for the frustration and helplessness my mother endured. I thought it was because of me that my mom and dad often fought. And so it became my Herculean effort to protect them from all of this at the age I was just learning to tie my shoes. I learned to hide my pain well, to swallow my rage at what was being done to me, and thus spare them the pain of witnessing me suffer. Doing so allowed me to be brutalized and degraded and to then get off the table, smile, and say, "Thank you for having me." This set in motion an all-too-familiar dynamic that has played itself out time and again in adulthood when, in escaping the violence of some abusive partner, I might look at the angry red welts rising in the mirror and think it wasn't so bad.

My early years were a dichotomy of hospital horrors and white bread banality. We lived in a quintessential tract house complete with a white picket fence on a tree-lined, shady street in the lofty "El Dorado Estates" development. In the endless California summer, I played with my Matchbox cars on the sidewalk until the streetlights came on and lazed on bean bag chairs with my neighborhood friends.

Once in a while, my father gave me a quarter to travel around the corner into Hawaiian Gardens to Giacopuzzi's dairy store on bustling Norwalk Boulevard to select an ice cream or a cold soda. Hawaiian Gardens was a mysterious otherworld of crime and urban blight. Tiny houses with bars on the windows lined narrow alleys filled with exotic, swarthy men in white t-shirts who hovered around lowered cars and played loud music. I didn't understand what any of this meant but I found it fascinating and alluring, a curiosity that became eroticized in my teens and led to much trouble in my adult years. It was in Hawaiian Gardens where my taste for bad boys and rough trade was born. I was never allowed into Hawaiian Gardens alone and never at night. At the time, the town boasted the most gang-affiliated Latino men per capita in the United States and the Crips had a stronghold as well. One of my most vivid childhood memories is of my father shoving me down onto the floor of the car as bullets sailed through the parking lot as we backed out of the Mexican barber shop and into the crossfire of the never-ending Hawaiian Gardens gang warfare.

My mother grew up in Detroit in a German and Polish immigrant community off 6 Mile Road at the height of the city's Motown era and crippling racial unrest. As a young girl, she swore she would "get the hell out of Detroit, but not," she added, "on the coattails of no man." Weekend charm school classes led to a lucrative modeling career with Revlon and ultimately, American Airlines and her ticket out of town. In addition to being a great beauty, my mother was a strong and independent thinker with a love for the written word. My mom stayed up each night devouring a new book, just finishing as the sun's first rays lit up her bedroom.

My father endured a hardscrabble Depression-Era childhood on the Great Plains of the American West. Homelessness and hardship were not unfamiliar to the large family of Swedish and Norwegian immigrants who made their living collecting scrap metal or logging. My dad joined the Air Force in 1958 and was stationed in Korea and Vietnam before joining American Airlines in 1965.

My parents were introduced at a party in Chicago in 1965 but my mom did not give my father a second glance, as she had just been awarded a transfer to the Washington, D.C., crew base and had rented an apartment with another stewardess there and was about to move in. My mother contracted Hepatitis B on a Mexico City trip a few days later and was ordered on bed rest. She returned to Detroit to rest under the watchful care of my grandmother, a retired nurse. When my father heard about my mother's predicament, he offered to make the move for her and got her set up in her new place while she recuperated. My dad soon transferred to Washington as well, and they were married about a year later. Although my mom was third in seniority in Washington, they transferred to Los Angeles where my father was awarded a position on the long-range Boeing 707 jetliner. They took a little apartment in Playa del Rey and set their sights on buying a home in neighboring Long Beach where the revolutionary new widebody DC-10 was under production.

I was six years old when my father started flying the 747 as a first officer. He took me on one of his New York City trips and I had the time of my life sitting in First Class and running up and down the spiral staircase to the opulent upper deck lounge where I sipped ginger ale with worldly sophistication. New York to a six-year-old was a new world of lights, people, and energy.

The return flight was American's prestigious Flight 21, with a lavish dinner service that was the height of airborne elegance. I sat regally in seat 1A, in the nose of the majestic airliner, as we lifted off the runway at JFK and into the night sky. About an hour into the flight it got quite choppy, and proceeded to get progressively rougher as we traveled west. Soon, the turbulence escalated significantly and the flight attendants were told to take their seats and strap in. We had entered an area of tornadoes and thunderstorms that spanned the Midwest. Ahead, a solid wall of severe weather lay in front of us, nearly impenetrable. The turbulence bordered on severe and there were several sharp drops and jolts as we soldiered through. Flight attendants in the aft became airsick, and the passengers were terrified. The rough ride lasted for hours, and no smooth air was found until Denver.

Yet ensconced in seat 1A, where I could see some of the sky ahead owing to the curvature of the aircraft's nose, I was having the time of my life watching the aircraft's navigation lights flash red against the broiling clouds as the 747 undulated and lumbered through the night. I thought the sound of flatware crashing to the floor and gasps of startled passengers to be the very soundtrack of adventure and excitement. When the pull-down movie screen at the front of the cabin bent and could not be retracted back into the ceiling, I didn't find it an unusual affair.

In fact, never once did it occur to me to feel fear because, in my six-year-old's mind, my daddy was clearly in command of the ship, and was doing exactly what he was best at doing at home: fixing things. I had never seen fear nor hesitation in my dad's eyes, and the idea that there should be anything to be afraid of with him around would have been unimaginable. I felt completely protected and comforted by his presence in the cockpit just a few feet above. What had been a night of living hell for so many grown-ups onboard had been a fantastic thrill-ride for a young boy to brag about at school the next day. My dad even made mention of that night in his retirement speech twenty years later, and I would speak of it at his funeral as a testament to his presence in my life as a source of support, comfort, and protection.

In the late 1960s, a bucolic farm town nestled in tree-dappled, rolling hills began to attract the attention of airline pilots guiding their jets overhead on approach to LAX. Thousand Oaks was known for its ideal, year-round climate.

To the airline pilots of the '60s, the town sat perched on the horizon as a Utopian alternative to the fast-encroaching urban sprawl that was quickly choking off the Los Angeles basin in a maze of sluggish freeways and brown smog. Equally compelling, Thousand Oaks was rated the Safest City in America, which was a selling point with the pilots' wives. Indeed, so many airline families relocated to the Conejo Valley that by the '70s, the town was often referred to as Thousand Pilots.

Against my mother's objections, my father purchased ten acres of undevelopable land on a steep grade five miles beyond town in 1977. Unbeknownst to my father, Ventura County was home to the most stringent zoning regulations in the country and the planning commission was notoriously anti-development, especially when the developers were interlopers from big-city Los Angeles set upon running roughshod over the rustic charm the city was keen to preserve.

We moved into a rambling ranch house on a cul-de-sac while my father went to work on his development scheme. My mother loathed Thousand Oaks from first sight, finding it sleepy and provincial. She missed her circle of friends back in Long Beach and soon fell into a deep depression, crying on the phone in her bedroom with her girlfriends for hours at a time.

My father, the few nights a week he was home, either hunkered over his blueprints for the house he hoped to build or reached for one of the endless, clanging liquor bottles in the cabinet above the refrigerator. Many nights, I lay in bed and listened to my parents' raised voices from the front room followed by the slam of the bedroom door.

Then came the plink of ice in a glass as my father settled in for a long night of drinking.

Life now split into two separate realities: when Dad was home, and when Dad went flying. When my father was away, life was good. Mom came out of her room and we would venture out of the driveway and do a little shopping or see a movie. Within a couple hours of my father pulling back into the driveway, however, battle stations were drawn. My mother would attempt a dinner in which my father would show little interest, preferring to drink instead. My mother would throw the food into the waste bin, slam the dishes into the dishwasher, and begin scrubbing the countertops, tightlipped and clench- jawed. My father would retreat to the living room to watch the news and proceed to drink himself into a stupor. Harsh words would ensue and my mother would throw something across the living room before stomping down the hall and slamming the bedroom door. I would then float bewildered in the long hallway down the middle of the house, feeling stricken and nauseous.

Eventually, I would run to my room and close my door as softly as possible. Once inside, I would listen to a record through my headphones and climb inside my closet to lose myself in my books, especially my airplane books (of which I had a vast collection). I looked at the pictures of the Lufthansa 707s and Pan Am 747s and imagine flying far away from all the anger and sadness. I lost myself in a fantasy world of elegance and sophistication, imagining myself a well-heeled passenger seated in the First Class cabin of a European-bound Boeing, surrounded by cosmopolitan and worldly fellow travelers. I could spend the entire night lost in my reverie and it wasn't too long before I started to wonder if my escapist daydreams might actually someday make for a practical plan of escape.

My father was one of six siblings and came from a religious family with a legacy of service in the mission field. One sister served Kenya for many years and the other married a pastor and raised her family while serving in India. Having family across the globe made for some fantastic travel opportunities.

One such exceptional trip was a round-the-world adventure with an extended family visit in Southern India. The journey began with a Pan Am flight from San Francisco to Narita, Japan, with an overnight stopover in Honolulu. At Narita, we connected to Hong Kong, landing just after dark at the famous Kai Tak Airport making the famous "checkerboard" approach which scraped the rooftops and shook the nearby buildings to their foundations. Hong Kong was dynamic and bustling with its unparalleled bargain shopping and sumptuous dining. Neon blazed and throngs of people darted to and fro like schools of fish. I stood mesmerized at the rail of the Star Ferry in the cool, humid breeze as we passed venerable junks and sampans then rode the tram up to Victoria Peak to gaze awestruck over the clamoring, mist-shrouded skyline as it pierced the silver sky. The ornate and decadent jumbo floating restaurant with its opulent dining room brimming with rich, intricately carved teak appointments awash in dazzling golds and fiery reds, was breathtaking.

Back at Kai Tak, we boarded an Air France 747 and flew to Bangkok, a seductive and steamy tropical paradise beneath a canopy of lush, leafy green. We marveled from an outboard motorboat at the myriad of narrow, twisting waterways that led to the bustling floating market filled with a cacophonous, screeching crescendo of animated and agitated back-and-forth haggling. Old, feisty women in wide-brimmed hats passed bags of rice between boats under the shade of broad and droopy trees laced with sinewy hanging vines. Along the riverbanks, lumbering gray elephants hoisted logs in their sturdy trunks and a tall and thin, toothless man charmed a thick cobra from a giant reed basket with the sound of his flute as I soaked it all in with wide-eyed wonder.

Another Air France jet carried us to Bombay. Outside baggage claim, the airport roadway was choked with traffic and smog and chaos and noise, and I found it utterly fascinating. A crowd stood gathered around a man with a small brown bear on a leash wearing a pink tutu. The little bear danced in circles for the cheering crowd. I moved in for a closer look but my mother yanked me back firmly by the hand.

"White slavery. They'd love to get their hands on a little blond boy here," my other scolded, clicking her tongue. I had no idea what she was talking about. I just wanted to pet the cute bear in a tutu.

Next, we boarded the brand new Airbus A-300 flown by Indian Airlines for a flight to Bangalore. Rich, deep gold and green colors adorned the cabin and we were welcomed warmly by the beautiful and gracious Indian flight attendants in bright gold and orange saris. After takeoff, a savory and aromatic Indian menu was served accompanied by fruit juice and coconut milk. We arrived just after dark following a beautiful sunset.

We rented a car and driver and headed toward Agra and the fabled Taj Mahal. Approaching the sacred site, one is struck by the hushed stillness in the air. The edifice is basked in a soft and hazy, ethereal light and enveloped in a silent peace as the river gently meanders without hurry nearby. It is timeless and eternal in its august and celestial presence. There is a comforting reverence in the air upon entering the cool shade of its pristine marble and it invites one to stop and rest awhile beneath its grandeur.

Heading back to Agra in the late afternoon, we passed through miles of gently rolling, green countryside dotted with silvery ponds reflecting billowy, white clouds on their mirrored faces. Graceful women wearing saris of vibrant colors hoisted to their knees waded out into the shallow water, carrying baskets and gliding between lily pads bearing bright white blossoms. A sweet, smoky scent hung in the air as fires were lit to prepare the evening's meal, casting a hazy, brownish-gray tint to the horizon ahead. The heady and piquant scent of curry and coconut wafted on the air from lantern-lit roadside stalls. Approaching each new town, the road became congested with rickety bicycles, ox-drawn carts, and whiny mopeds, a dizzying and swirling vortex of humanity and the chaos of nightfall.

The next day, we arrived at the home of my aunt and uncle, situated on the mission station just outside of town. The compound was a small, self-contained village of its own, consisting of a comfortable yet understated church and meeting hall, a respectable schoolhouse, and small, humble homes for missionaries, students, and groundsmen and their families. Stables and a small farm provided for the nutritional needs of the station. It was a rudimentary yet hospitable, efficient organization with the needs of the people it served as its primary focus and function.

We stayed at the mission station for two weeks and met many of the seminary students and members of the congregation. In the adjacent village, we were warmly welcomed into the austere and often ramshackle homes which tightly lined deeply rutted, muddy lanes. Many of the structures were without front doors and even roofs and we sat gathered in a circle, often on low, threadbare sofas, on the floor, or occasionally on plastic milk crates sipping tea or fruit juice served with the greatest of formality. Yet our hosts were always house-proud and so generous with what little they had, often going without themselves to ensure that we were content. On occasion, a cow might push its way inside the open doorway and wander around the house listing about aimlessly. It was explained that in India, the cow was considered sacred and thus granted carte blanche to go where he pleased.

Wherever we went in the village, we attracted a huge throng of onlookers and followers, mostly children. It was very overwhelming to have 15–20 people swarm us everywhere we went, crowding suffocatingly close, touching us, and tugging at our clothing while shrieking rapidly in a frightening language. Most were beggars, their hands outstretched and demanding, their voices raised, becoming angry and indignant when we did not respond. At one point, we became separated from my aunt and were so mobbed that my mother clutched my hand tightly and dragged me toward the car, both of us near tears. She opened the door and threw me inside, slamming the door behind us. I looked up to a sea of angry, expectant faces pressed up against the glass and I buried my face in my mother's side and cried. The mob banged their palms and fists against the glass, jeering, and the car began rocking from side to side. Finally, my mother struck back, slapping the glass with her open palm with such force that everyone outside froze and took a sharp breath inward. Then at once, they all screamed in unison and ran away from the savage woman.

To make matters worse, huddled in the backseat, cowering beneath my mother's raincoat, my head began to spin and a wave of nausea washed over me and I soon threw up, much to the excitement of the voyeurs who had now returned to the window.

Back at the house, my mother and aunt spoke urgently in hushed tones outside my room about an illness that had been taking a toll on the village children. A child with similar symptoms had died in the village that week. I was terribly sick by now with a high fever and horrific stomach cramps and I couldn't hold anything down. A doctor came from town and something was prescribed which went a long way in easing my malaise. The medication—combined with bananas, rice pudding, and coconut milk—had me rallying in a few days. The most pointed medical advice, however, was that we should leave India straight away. The night before we left, another child died in the village of the mystery illness.

Although a child, I was made painfully and acutely aware of the tragic disparity between my experience of this illness and that of the more vulnerable kids dying just down the way in the village. Until India, I had not known I existed in a world of haves and have-nots. This was new information to me, and my experience left me a very sad seven-year-old. This ordeal opened my eyes to social injustice and economic inequality. I am thankful to my parents, who believed travel to be the best form of education, and who did not shield me from its unpleasant realities but instead, showed me the world in all its glitter and gore.

For all the wonderful opportunities afforded by growing up in the airline industry, there were dark moments as well. The airline community is close-knit. When something goes wrong, it ripples across the industry in a most profound way.

My mother picked me up early from school one morning. She told me that there had been an accident, that an airplane had crashed but that it was not my father's. She wanted to make sure I understood that my dad was safe. It was May 25th, 1979, and American Airlines flight 191, a DC-10, had crashed on takeoff from Chicago's O'Hare Airport.

The flight was headed for Los Angeles with three pilots—eight San Diego, and two Los Angeles-based flight attendants aboard. The aircraft was carrying 258 passengers. There were no survivors. As a senior DC-10 first officer, my dad was a regular on the Chicago-Los Angeles route and was, in fact, at that moment on a layover at a hotel in Chicago preparing to work the next day's Flight 191 back to Los Angeles.

The next 24 hours were anxious and sad. The phone rang constantly and flying friends stopped by in various states of shock to exchange news or console one another. The heart-stopping image of the stricken jetliner balanced on one wing just before nosing down into the field and exploding into a giant fireball glared back from the muted television in the front room. My dad arrived home grave and somber the next day and immediately closed himself off in his office while on the phone with his union and fellow pilots.

My father had been one of American's first DC-10 pilots and had been trained by McDonnell Douglas in Long Beach. With his tremendous knowledge of the aircraft and its systems, he was in demand for his expertise in light of the tragedy. He immediately joined the investigating committee and began researching what brought the aircraft down—specifically, what part training and cockpit procedures may have played in the chain of events leading up to the crash. The cockpit crew of Flight 191 had done everything right. They followed their training and procedures to the letter under unimaginable conditions and extreme stress. Unfortunately, those procedures may have sealed their fate and this weighed heavily upon my dad. I am incredibly proud of my father and his role in ensuring that American, his pilot colleagues, and the DC-10 remained the hallmark of aviation safety.

Within days, the manifest containing familiar names was released and a new sadness descended upon the house. The aircraft was under the command of three veteran pilots my father respected greatly and my mother had fond memories of flying with several of the flight attendants herself. The next few days were confusing and lonely as I wandered up and down the hallway, listening at the doors as my father worked the investigation from his office and my mother cried on the phone with her former flying partners mourning their losses. This left me lost and alone, trying to make sense of this new, sad reality that was now my home life. As my parents' friends were mostly fellow American Airlines pilots and flight attendants past and present, it seemed the crash was all anyone talked about.

For many airline industry families, especially those at American Airlines, the Flight 191 disaster was, without a doubt, the end of the innocence of the high flying '70s.

CHAPTER 2

In the 1970s, the Dallas Cowboys came to Thousand Oaks for training camp each summer, setting the town abuzz. I was about seven, riding my bike with a few friends when we passed a nondescript house in the neighborhood. "Hey, you know that's where the Cowboys stay, don't you? Let's see what they're up to," my friend Jerry called out.

We laid our bikes down on the driveway and knocked on the door. A hulking African-American man opened the door and greeted us with amusement. He motioned us in, shrugged, and turned to walk back down the hall, leaving us to ourselves in the front room. We looked around the house for a bit, examining its contents reverently as if in a museum. After a few minutes, Jerry beckoned us down the hallway to a room where a few spectacularly robust players sat around a television watching an afternoon movie. He walked over to the black man, whispered something in his ear, then smiled at the rest of us standing in the doorway. Once back in the living room, Jerry announced proudly, "He says we can look at the Playboys."

I had never seen anything racier than a *National Geographic* before that day and the centerfolds made my blood race. But it was the room mere feet away filled with prime examples of the male species that made my head spin. I found myself caught in the hallway floating between two worlds, my head swimming with water boy fantasies. That was the day I first realized my tastes might be just a little different than those of my little friends. It never occurred to me to ask my friend how he knew there was a house just down the block filled with Dallas Cowboys with a stack of Playboys on the coffee table. As an adult, this raises all kinds of questions but at the time, I thought I had struck gold.

When I was eleven, I made a discovery that would alter the course of my life irrevocably. *The Sexual Outlaw: A Documentary: A Nonfiction Account, with Commentaries, of Three Days and Nights in the Sexual Underground*, chronicled the wild and wanton sexual adventures of a young, gay man immersed in the gay cruising scene of Los Angeles in the 1970s, and read like a how-to manual for sourcing casual and anonymous sex.

I tore into the tome and read it cover to cover in one sitting then promptly headed out on my Huffy dirt bike to recreate as many scenes as I could with this titillating new information. In no time, I found a host of venues where men gathered for clandestine sexual encounters and within hours, I was the toast of a loose-knit community of hungry and depraved sexual predators, older men in their 40s, 50s, and 60s, eagerly awaiting a young boy possessed by an intoxicating combination of surging hormones and morbid curiosity.

My first sexual encounter with a man took place within hours at the public library and was perhaps one of the most traumatic of my life. From the book, I learned about public sex and the well-rehearsed choreography involved in signaling oneself available and selecting a partner in a highly trafficked place. The man I met was drunk and aggressive and his breath reeked of alcohol and cigarettes. I was reviled. He had a leering, penetrating stare that froze me in my tracks. And while I didn't know quite what to expect when I started the adventure, clearly this was not who I was looking for. In the ultimate of clichés, he said he had a van parked outside and kept drunkenly insisting I join him in it. The idea terrified me to the core yet the more I demurred, the more frustrated he became, and I saw the flash of anger in his eyes. My years of training to be a good and compliant patient, to allow frightening adults to do what they would to my body, served me this time as a survival skill. Instead, I persuaded him to guide me into a nearby field, choosing the lesser of two evils. I did not know what would happen in the expansive field hidden by trees and brush, far from the building. I quickly realized this would not be the erotic adventure I sought when I started this exploit, but rather a violation I would have to endure and somehow survive. Despite my strong and primal urge to turn and run, I felt my body plodding on towards my inevitable fate as if in a trance, unable to will my limbs to carry me in another direction.

Once under the cover of a shady oak, he sat down on a fallen log and motioned me to join him. I sat down tentatively and terrified, looking straight ahead, my heart in my throat. He unbuttoned his corduroy pants and exposed himself to me. I was horrified and intrigued and aroused and nauseated all at once. His fully-developed, adult genitalia fascinated me but his slurred speech, hateful and penetrating glare, and the reek of alcohol turned my stomach.

He kept insisting I touch him. I kept delaying and resisting until he finally reached out and grabbed my hand roughly, and shoved it down his open pants. He was hot and sticky and wet and I was repulsed and fascinated and I wanted to scream while still reaching deeper. He was angry now, tired of my hesitancy and games. For a second, I wondered if I would die.

Suddenly, he grabbed me roughly and jerked me to face him. He clawed at the waistband of my shorts and underpants and tugged them down, tearing the button off my shorts in the process. I gasped, then froze, paralyzed in terror, unable to move.

I stood there, naked from the waist down, exposed and bare and horrified, as his rough hands violated me. He stared at me defiantly, holding my gaze with a burning, hate-filled scowl as if issuing an unspoken threat or dare. My head swam and my face went flush. This was wrong. So very, very wrong. This was not what I wanted at all. I had made a huge mistake. In the distance, traffic passed on the freeway. Birdsong carried on the warm summer air. I wanted to scream out, to run. Yet, I stood perfectly still, allowing his unfettered exploration of my pubescent body. I felt myself shutting down, turning inward, and I became an inanimate object. I willed my heart to stop pounding and my breath to slow to a shallow pant. I stared at a point straight ahead as my peripheral vision went dark. I detached and I simply endured.

And when he finished, I rose, pulled up my pants quickly, and began to back away leaving him there by the fallen tree. My heart thundered in my temples and I thought my legs would give way at any moment. I needed to be in the comfort and security of my parents' house at once. I wanted to cry out for help as I passed the busy and distracted people heading into the library but I had done this horrific thing, invited this appalling deed, and worse, part of me wanted more.

I jumped on my bicycle and I pedaled as fast as I could towards home. Halfway, I was overcome with a violent rage. With each block traveled, I grew more vengeful, more hostile toward this vile and vulgar man who had frightened and objectified me so and rendered me powerless. I pulled over at a payphone in front of a Safeway supermarket, dialed 0 for the operator, and asked for the police. It took three tries to stammer out that I had just come from the library and that a man was touching children there. The dispatcher couldn't be less interested. All she wanted to know was my name, which she asked me three times. When I refused to give it to her, she said dourly, "Well I can't take a report if I don't have your name." When she asked me where I was at that moment, I hung up in a panic. I stood there reeling. I felt like I had been punched in the stomach and I wandered back to my bicycle feeling lost and abandoned and utterly alone. I pedaled my bicycle up into the garage, ran past my father and into the kitchen and all the way down the hallway into the bathroom, slamming the door behind me. I looked at myself in the mirror. My face was flushed, and I was panting, breathless. Then I laid down on the floor and curled myself up in the throw rug, squinting my eyes closed and wishing it all away. I went back to the library the next day, and most every day for the next three years.

I quickly fell into a pattern of acting out sexually and compulsively with older men most days. They were disembodied penises, masculine limbs and torsos to touch and admire but not faces, and certainly, never eyes. The hate-filled, penetrating glare of that first vulgar man and my defilement at his rough and brusque hands had traumatized me far too deeply to make more than fleeting eye contact with anyone else again. Besides, to hold my gaze for more than an instant was to broach questions, questions deep within myself I had no answers to. And yet, there were urgent, pressing questions that needed to be asked. It might have occurred to one or two of the married fathers who exploited me each day to ask what a twelve-year-old boy was doing in a back alley sucking off seven married men each day. Yet somehow, it never came up. In fact, I rarely received even a word of greeting before getting it on, let alone a single word of concern.

There were, however, occasional men who inquired about my age, or asked if I were eighteen prior to fucking me. These men asked not out of concern for my welfare, but to assuage their guilt and to steer clear of the law. Pedophiles covering their asses before taking mine in stride. I found myself in a field surrounded by three middle-aged men wearing wedding rings, dicks in hand, leering at me hungrily. "Put the kid in the middle," one lecher rasped. I despised these men passionately as I knelt obediently on the sun-cracked ground.

Over the years, there was a small handful of men I saw on an occasional basis. They were friendly, light, and generous in the bedroom. They each tried to draw me out, but I was too traumatized and overwhelmed to engage much beyond our physical exchanges and despite their awkward attempts at stilted conversation, I generally just sat in the front seat looking nervously ahead as they drove us to their apartments. Yet our encounters were more than merely transactional, and I did not feel so used and objectified with these men as I often did in my purely anonymous encounters elsewhere. I looked forward to the company of these rare men, and felt relieved when I saw one of them pull up in his car. These men were sensual and unhurried, relaxed and open. They inspired and nurtured my curiosity and they seemed to respect my need to set the pace for it. They were not the typical married pedophiles I was so regularly exploited by, but rather openly gay men living independent, single lives and therefore, free to indulge as they pleased. We were not engaging under severe time constraints or the dread of discovery, just enjoying the evening and my newly-emerging sexuality as it unfolded.

And there were too the occasional standout experiences that left me feeling appreciated, validated, and satisfied. At sixteen, I traveled to Mexico City with my father where I gave him the slip for a couple hours, anxious to meet a tall, dark Latin man, which I easily found in the Zocalo. His name was Enrique and he was masculine and virile, yet kind and gentle, and particularly concerned with my well-being alone on the streets of the Capital. He shepherded me into a nearby bar to question me, then offered me a drink. I declined, and had a 7-Up instead. We sat and chatted for a while in English and Spanish before he made a very formal and gentlemanly offer of intimacy at his apartment. With his hand on the small of my back, he guided me down a narrow, cobblestone alleyway, through a wooden gate, and into a magical tiled courtyard filled with riotous jacaranda and bougainvillea. We passed into a cozy, low-slung apartment and once behind the closed door, he took my face in his warm, strong hands and kissed me gently, then began biting my lips playfully. He was giving and patient, sensual yet strong, and when it was over, he insisted on walking me back to my father's door. He bowed to me reverently as I slipped the key in the lock, then disappeared down the corridor and out of my life.

These men, both the married pedophiles and the intriguing, intoxicating partners I rushed to meet clandestinely, were adults decades my senior in both life and experience. Thus, the onus of propriety and responsibility was on them. It would take decades of therapy to understand that for these grown men to engage in sexual relations with me, a child, regardless of what I did or didn't think I wanted at the time, was wrong, period.

This point was driven home in a particularly jarring and salient fashion when my therapist looked at me one day and asked, "Could YOU fuck a twelve-year-old?" Of course I couldn't and certainly wouldn't, but why had they?

In therapy, I learned about human growth and sexual development and the reason the law stands as it does. I now understand that the body and mind do not always develop in synchronicity. A young person, a boy in particular, may become physically capable of sexual behavior long before his mind is able to wrap itself around all that comes with it. I was in no way prepared for the emotional fallout of the behaviors in which I was engaging in nor the social and emotional complexities they brought. I did not have the tools to navigate through the moral implications and potential legal and health ramifications of my actions. This left me overloaded and lost, and ultimately paralyzed.

The truth is, regardless of what I thought I wanted, I simply wasn't ready for sex with anyone, let alone the furtive and shameful objectification which substituted for the guidance, mentoring, and encouragement I so desperately needed at those ages.

Having no one to discuss these difficult experiences with, I turned to journaling to purge myself of painful and overwhelming feelings. I spent much of the day at my desk trying to write my way out of tricking, then once I had inevitably succumbed, I would creep home in a veil of shame and remorse and spend hours trying to make sense of what had just occurred, chronicling all the gory details in a series of spiral-bound notebooks. Each day was filled with basically the same entry with slight variations for characters and venues over the course of three or four years of acting out.

I was fifteen when I climbed into a van in the parking lot of a local park on a wintery afternoon and joined the driver, a grandfatherly man in his mid-60s, in the front seat. He felt me up asked if I would like to come back to his place. I was not attracted to the man in the least but the idea of heading somewhere warm and discreet appealed to me so I accepted the invitation.

He pulled onto the road and began chatting nervously, asking a myriad of questions about my experience and sexual tastes. I was too paranoid for conversation so I sat silently with my hands folded. Thankfully, it was only a few miles' drive before he pulled through the gates of a mobile home park, stopping in front of a double-wide trailer in the middle of a quiet lane. On my side and only a few feet away, a man stood hunched under the raised hood of a car, working on the engine intently. I noticed my host stiffen and grip the wheel tighter. He told me that he did not think the man would see us, but if he were to ask, I was to say that I was the son of a coworker. Instantly, I felt a pang of guilt shoot through me. It was a flimsy explanation, and I began to panic, knowing the neighbor's attention and curiosity were inevitable. I stepped down lightly, keeping my eyes fixed on the front door, and walked quickly up the stairs in front of my host. For what felt like a lifespan, I stood frozen on the sagging porch staring straight ahead while my host nervously struggled with the lock before cracking the door open and ushering me quickly inside the darkened trailer.

Once inside, I looked around and surveyed the home. The dated interior boasted shag carpet and faux wood paneling on the walls. A clunky, well-worn sofa loomed against one wall. The man motioned to it and invited me to sit. He offered me a beer and I declined, assuming we would head straight to the bedroom and get to the business at hand. Instead, he popped the cap off a bottle for himself and sat down in a wooden chair adjacent and began prodding me with more questions, trying to get me to relax and unwind. I had not come for conversation and I just wanted the whole affair over already. But the man continued to prattle on, desperately attempting to engage me despite my obvious disinterest and distress. After what seemed an eternity, he finished his beer, rose, and beckoned me into the bedroom. He left the lights on full which made me flood with self-consciousness. We began to undress on opposite sides of the bed and I laid down on the mattress and turned my head to regard the room dispassionately.

My gaze fell on the nightstand upon which a greeting card stood next to a single, withering red rose in a vase. The man stepped into the bathroom which gave me a quick second to examine the card closer. To my horror, it was an anniversary card. The flowery script inside professed love and gratitude for 40-some years of marital bliss. It was signed, "Yours, Yvonne." I felt as though I had been slapped in the face as a wave of nausea washed over me followed by a surge of anger and bitterness.

He was heavy and unskilled, dead weight and insisted on trying to keep up the one-sided banter in the brightly lit room, now with the introduction of pet names. Stuck on foreplay, he fondled and caressed ad nauseum and delayed moving on, as if to prolong the ordeal. I went through the motions wanly and rotely, slack and lifeless, wishing I were anywhere else but in a threadbare double-wide with this oafish, unfaithful lout, and kept chanting, "I'm sorry" into the universe as if to somehow ease the aggrieved wife, whom I expected to storm into the home at any moment. I was many things, but I was not a teenage homewrecker. An aching sadness for the long suffering spouse and her shitty lot in life washed over me.

When we finally snuck back down the front steps several hours later, there was no sight of the neighbor nor his broken down car, by the grace of God. We drove in silence this time, each spiraling into our own brooding, personal darkness, back to the park where he let me off at the front gate and drove away at top speed.

Back home, showered, and locked safely behind my bedroom door, I pulled out one of the spiral notebooks and began to write about the adulterous encounter, emphasizing the horrifying moment I reached over and absently picked up the card congratulating the man on over forty years of faithful marriage.

I awoke late the next morning and ran out the door without first locking up the notebook as I usually did. When I arrived home a few hours later, I found my mother sitting in the living room with a tear-stained face, holding the journal in her lap. Mistaking it for schoolwork I had left behind, she had flipped through it to see what I was working on in class, and had gotten quite an education herself.

I felt the breath leave my chest and the room went dark as I heard myself whispering "No" in a weak and plaintive voice as the room began to spin. I staggered to a chair and landed heavily on it, wishing anything but this present moment.

She asked if I were practicing some creative writing, if perhaps this were some erotic fiction I was working on. I couldn't respond. She then asked point-blank if I were gay.

A wave of desperation and panic washed over me and I protested adamantly that it was just something that had happened once in a while that I was working hard on changing. I promised it wouldn't happen again. She questioned how I could have pulled all of this off without her or my father catching wind or without getting myself arrested, and reminded me that my behavior was highly illegal. She said she was shocked to learn that such things happened in public. Above all, she was sad that she had missed this, that I could be going through so much and she never knew. The pain on my mother's face was heartbreaking. I carried my secret as long as I had out of fear and concern for my parents. I believed this would be more than they could handle. The shame and remorse I felt in the moment was more for what I believed I was doing to my parents than anything else.

We sat quietly together in sad and awkward silence until she asked me what I wanted to do about it all. I said I didn't know and that I had been trying to "quit" for some time unsuccessfully. She said she would have to tell my father about this of course, and that we would all discuss it together when he got home from his trip. She reassured me that they would find some help for me, which did bring some relief. However, the thought of reliving this appalling conversation across the table from my aloof and stoic, homophobic father who loved a good gay joke, was more than I could bare. I said I needed to lay down.

I excused myself from the room then ran down the hall at full speed, directly into the bathroom, locking the door behind me. I crumpled to my knees begging God to take this moment from me, to take me back just a day in time so that I could avert this disaster. But I knew there could be no return from this horror, and nausea clutched my stomach. I turned on the bathtub faucet hoping the noise from the tap would drown out my dire thoughts and abject misery. I laid down on the throw rug and curled into a fetal pose and felt my heart shatter into a thousand pieces as tears spilled from my eyes.

Then it occurred to me that there was a bottle of Benadryl capsules in the cabinet above. One Benadryl capsule always knocked me out for a night and so I wondered if perhaps a whole bottle could put me to sleep forever.

I felt a profound sadness coupled with an unbearable, aching loneliness. I stood, opened the cabinet, and removed the bottle. I unscrewed the top and peered inside. It was nearly full and I knew there was more than enough to do the job with a few to spare. Hurriedly, I poured the pills into my hand and rolled them back and forth in my palm. They were cool and light against my flesh. I felt release and peace again. Then I poured them gently back into the bottle, replaced the cap, and put the bottle back in the cabinet. I laid back down on the throw rug and wrapped myself up in it tightly. I closed my eyes and listened to the din of the running faucet. The sound of the water splashing in the tub echoed off the tiles and reverberated around the room, comforting me burrowed in my insular rug on the cold floor. I prayed to God and asked for His forgiveness one last time. Forgiveness for all I had done with the many men I had seduced, and forgiveness for this unspeakable thing I now considered that would cause my parents an unbearable anguish from which they would never recover.

CHAPTER 3

I sat across from the psychoanalyst in his sumptuously appointed office, feeling hopeful. Dr. Karasic looked like Sigmund Freud and Mr. Rogers in one. He explained that he had a basic understanding of my case from his meeting with my parents earlier and he said he thought he could help me. He asked me if I thought I was a "homosexual." I recoiled in terror. "Of course not," I objected. "I just can't stop having sex with men," I explained, tearfully. He considered this and then asked me to tell him in my own words what was happening. I pushed through my embarrassment to outline my daily battle against overwhelming sexual desire and the invariable failure of willpower which led to such shame and remorse and my wanting to end my life.

When I finished my lengthy dissertation, he said he was fairly certain that I was in the grips of a strong compulsive disorder. He explained a little bit about the subconscious and about the psychoanalytic process. He told me that the subconscious was a powerful force and explained how thoughts we weren't aware of deep within the mind influenced our behaviors. He explained that once revealed and brought to the light of day, these hidden thoughts lost their power. Therefore, he claimed, it was just a matter of rooting through my unconscious until we hit upon the magic bullet that was driving me to such behavior. Once revealed, my subconscious' power over my life would dissipate, and my conscious willpower and self-determination would prevail once more. I would be free.

He said we were very fortunate that we had caught my behavior early enough in my sexual development. We could still find the subconscious root of my desire for sex with men and redirect it before it became permanently etched upon my psyche. Changing my sexual appetite, he explained, would be possible as long as I was willing to do the deep dive necessary to reach hidden thoughts in the subconscious. I would have to commit to complete transparency and I would have to lay myself completely bare to the process, no matter how painful or humiliating it became. The process would require scrutinous examination of my sexual fantasies in lurid detail. I would have to recount my every sexual escapade. There could be no privacy, only the glaring lens of the analyst's magnifying glass. I would know nothing but violation and invasion going forward.

I accepted readily that allowing this voyeuristic ghoul entree into my innermost private thoughts was the only modality that could lead to the normalcy I so desperately craved. I surrendered my boundaries gratefully that I might be the most compliant, pleasing, and therefore successful patient yet, and committed wholeheartedly to the mysterious and magical process of psychoanalytic conversion therapy.

Bastille Day, 1989, found me carefree and headstrong on a two-week solo vacation in Paris at seventeen years old. I wasted no time in finding love. Sinewy and chiseled, with black eyes that bored through my very soul when I first passed him on a rain-slicked street in the 18th arrondissement, his name was Phillipe and he lived in Montmartre, not far from the funicular. The nighttime Sacre Ceoure, ablaze in brilliant floodlights, filled the entire bedroom window and bathed the room in pale luminescence. From the street, the flat was the third from the left on the third floor overlooking the garden. The beauty and depth of Phillipe's heart would be precisely what broke mine to pieces when shortly into my first adult love affair he announced he was returning to Sub-Saharan Africa where he worked with the children of a refugee camp, a noble undertaking that only made me love him more. He left a few days before me, and I moved into a tiny hotel room on the Square d' Anvers where I cried my heart out as any teenager who has just lost his first love would do.

As I packed my bag on that last day, the concierge rang the room and told me that he had been holding a letter from Phillipe with instructions to deliver it on the day of my departure. It began "Tonight was so very difficult for us both." In his letter, Phillipe had written the most beautiful, poetic words about our time together along with some gentle talk about how I may have been somewhat susceptible to the charms of the City of Lights and a dark-eyed foreigner speaking the Language of Love. He worried about my not having anyone to talk about this side of myself once back home and offered his friendship and guidance from across the sea. His words, in elegant script on beautiful parchment, were like a balm to my soul, and I treasured them for years.

With the finality of the landing gear retracting into the underside of the Lufthansa 727 that lifted me up and away from Charles de Gaulle, I felt my heart shatter into a million pieces, knowing then, I would never feel Phillipe's gentle caress again.

Transiting Frankfurt, the true crossroads of the world, my spirits began to lift somewhat as I passed a dozen or more Pan Am 747s and A-310s and marveled at the sight of the worldly and polished flight crew gliding easily amongst the passengers from across the globe, some in turbans or flowing saris, and I vowed to return to Frankfurt in uniform myself. Climbing out a few hours later seated in my first First Class seat with my treasured letter clutched to my chest, I knew I would never be the same. I had known a glamorous, whirlwind love with a virile and confident, exotic man in the most seductive city in the world and become a man myself in the process. I had shed the bonds of sleepy Thousand Oaks, California. I had walked among cosmopolitan masses and heard languages from around the world. I had seen departure boards listing flights to places like Tirana, Geneva, Riyadh, and Nairobi. Never again could I be satisfied with the life I knew before, as I had experienced a true awakening that would inform my life from that moment on.

I returned to Thousand Oaks changed. Having seen the world beyond my backyard, I had lost interest in my small town and the small minds it contained. Plus, I was desperate to escape the clutches of Dr. Karasic. I set my sights on a career as a flight attendant, and enrolled in Spanish classes to up my chances of being selected with Pan Am. My escape plan was to get hired upon graduation and get based in London, as far away from Thousand Oaks as possible. If Pan Am wouldn't take me, I would apply with TWA or Northwest. All three airlines were big international carriers flying 747s. I was very specific in my requirements.

I took a part-time after-school job at J.C. Penney in the men's department in my senior year.

One night, a pretty, young sales associate came over to ask the price of an item. She was a knockout with beautiful, flowing blonde ringlets that framed her wide face and porcelain complexion and the most crystal blue, piercing eyes I'd ever seen. She had a throaty, hearty laugh and a raspy, low voice. She was glamorous, with confidence and a presence like I had never seen in a woman before. We introduced ourselves. Her name was Cynthia; she went to a rival crosstown high school.

We began spending time together and quickly started dating steadily. Soon, our relationship turned physical, and I lost my "straight" virginity. And just like that, I was cured. After three years of conversion therapy I was a heterosexual. All it took was one post-prom drunken romp and a promise ring and all was right in the world again. Dr. Karasic was so very thrilled and my treatment was terminated. My parents were thrilled. My friends were thrilled. The only one not ecstatic was me.

I had an anxious, unsettled feeling in the pit of my stomach most of the time. I felt like I had lost control, like I was on a runaway train. I loved being a couple, I loved the pet names, the companionship, the racing home from school and waiting for that phone call that lasted for hours. But, I just wanted to slow down. Cynthia was determined to nail me down any way she could. She talked about the future, about a family, and about marriage. She wanted a house right away. I loved all of those ideas, in theory at least, truly. But we were only graduating high school and I still had my heart set on flying.

I sent out 42 typed letters and resumes to every airline serving LAX during my senior year. I got one call back, from SkyWest Airlines. The woman who interviewed me a week before graduation was joyful and pleasant and told me she'd never interviewed someone still in high school. But I sold myself hard and she agreed to give me a shot. I started my training the day of my high school graduation, skipping my graduation ceremony to drive 65 miles to start training as a ticket agent instead.

I was now living with Cynthia and her mother and leaving the house at 4:30 every morning to be at the gate by 6 a.m. I would drive the 405 freeway home at rush hour and arrive exhausted, but I was living my dream of working for an airline. A number of the flight attendants were encouraging me to put in a transfer to In-Flight on my nineteenth birthday a few months away. It was a very exciting and hopeful time.

Then on the afternoon of February 1, 1991, I closed up a flight at gate 67, turned to my coworkers, and said goodbye. I had just walked through the door at home when I heard the report from the television that a US Air 737 and a SkyWest Metroliner had collided and were burning, ironically, against a fire station at LAX. My heart sank and I said a prayer for our passengers and crew, and spent a sleepless night watching the news as it unfolded.

Back at the airport in the morning, my supervisor asked me if I would escort and assist a gentleman whose brother had been killed in the crash, which I was honored to do. By sunrise, the smoldering wreckage was easily visible on the north side of the airport. In the days to come as the investigation began, the charred wreckage of the SkyWest aircraft was relocated to the hangar adjacent to the employee parking lot. Each day for a month we were insensitively and inhumanely subjected to the sight of charred fuselage, including the crushed seat frames and cockpit instrument panels, and the severed engines leaking fuel and hydraulic fluid across the hangar floor. Many of us knew the two pilots who were killed in the crash. This was the beginning of my aviation-related PTSD.

I transferred to In-Flight Services with SkyWest Airlines on my nineteenth birthday and headed out to training in Palm Springs. I began my flying career as a Salt Lake City-based flight attendant on the Brasilia turboprop aircraft. On the drive up to Salt Lake, Cynthia and I stopped in Las Vegas and got married in a late night ceremony on the Strip.

I loved the Inter-Mountain flying with its beautiful scenic vistas and small-town destinations. I soon transferred to Palm Springs where I flew an easy schedule that had me back by the pool by noon most days. Life was idyllic for a whole three months until I was unceremoniously furloughed when the company realized they had made a hiring mistake by bringing aboard three flight attendants younger than the Utah Alcoholic Beverage Commission allowed. Suddenly unemployed, we had no choice but to move back in with Cynthia's mother in California once more.

"Buried secretly and silently inside, is an achingly beautiful, devastating sorrow of which I can only catch fleeting glimpses. It is the sweetest grief, the most resplendent of mourning and it whispers my name in the most unexpected touch and go moments, turning my head and reminding me that sorrow, like a barren and craggy, frozen arctic fjord, possesses an ethereal beauty in the mist-shrouded first light of solitary morning."
– entry from Steven Slater's journal

Back in Moorpark in the trailer in the orchard, I fell into a sadness of a magnitude of which I had never known before. It seemed as though the very life had been drained from my body and spirit. Indeed, my spirit had been broken when my wings had been clipped.

It was all I could do to make it to the couch each morning and lay prone, the crushing weight on my chest so heavy I could not rise except to use the bathroom or occasionally eat, though I did that rarely. So profound was this sadness that all I did was cry softly throughout the day, my head turned, staring vacantly at the wall. It was as if the rug had been pulled from beneath my feet and I was falling farther and farther each day into an unsettling, anxious darkness. I could no longer see the light above me. In fact, I now preferred a darkened room, and kept the blinds closed once Cynthia left for work at the salon where she did nails to support us.

Under the suffocating weight of depression, the noise of the television hurt my ears and music sounded flat. Well-intended words of encouragement from friends only served to mock me and their joyful laughter pierced my heart, leaving me deflated and feeling worse. I lost my dream job in July but this spiral only deepened and careened further downward as autumn arrived. With February's gray skies came still darker thoughts. Clearly, this was more than just an adjustment period, but lost in the darkness, I could not find perspective on what was happening to my battered psyche nor ask for help—help I didn't know I desperately needed.

Cynthia had grown frustrated, feeling helpless in her inability to cajole me back to life. She tried admirably, rounding up our friends and planning evenings out, but I always begged off at the last minute.

I completely shut down in the bedroom as well, and this was a source of great frustration especially given the large role sex had played in our youthful relationship. She was a twenty-year-old new bride and while coming home had been a great shame and a sign of failure for me, she was thrilled to be back with her young girlfriends and soon began going out on the town with her old crew while I cried on the couch at home alone. Soon, she was running around Hollywood, hanging out in the Viper Room and other hot spots with a brazen and headstrong, self-possessed crew of young women who were not inclined to be held back by recently unemployed husbands sidelined by undiagnosed bipolar depression. Naturally, they attracted a lot of male attention wherever they went.

Cynthia tried to give our marriage all she could but faced with a completely disinterested and depressed partner, met her limits fairly soon. She was honest and transparent about what was going on in

Hollywood. She told me about the men she was meeting and the attention she was attracting. She told me about the flirtations and I gave her my blessing. I knew I was in no condition to run and play in the big city, even though I was filled with envy and jealousy. I wanted to be a part of it, but I could not get myself to the refrigerator and back, let alone to Sunset Boulevard.

It wasn't long before Cynthia told me about a young man she had been seeing. He was everything I was not: tall, Latino, athletic, and popular. We had many friends in common. It had been going on for a while, she explained. I was, at this point, the only one in our circles who did not know about the affair. I was humiliated and angry and hurt. I felt like a knife had been driven through my chest with the news and I thought back to the humiliation and shame that had descended over our home when my father confessed his infidelities and how I had never really recovered from the blow of my parents' divorce. Now, here I was reliving all of that in my own marriage at just twenty years old.

On some level, I was jealous of this affair, too. Although I was all-in with my marriage, there was another side of me that was vying for male attention. I longed for some masculine company of my own. It in no way negated what I had in my marriage but was rather an emerging desire that was making itself known after having been set aside for some time. It was not that I wanted either/or, to be gay or straight. It was that I wanted a bit of both, in a complementary manner. It was finally coming clear after so much struggle and denial and therapy and work, that I was bisexual.

I found a job at the Broadway department store, where I was quickly promoted to the management training program. While my career was on the rise, my marriage continued to decline. I could no longer tolerate the infidelity nor my own inauthenticity and unspoken need.

Cynthia and I had yet another fight about her relationship with the Latino boy and I said I needed some time away. I jumped in my car and headed north, with no destination in mind. Five hours later, I pulled into a motel in San Luis Obispo, feeling lighter and freer than I had in years. The open road had given me space to think, and I realized that what I really wanted was out.

I truly loved my wife but marriage just wasn't right for me. I was only twenty and I had gotten in over my head and married too soon. I still wanted to fly and I wasn't ready to settle down. Cynthia was obviously no longer invested in the marriage and there was no sense in delaying the inevitable. I vowed to make my case for divorce in the morning. That night, I slept better than I had in years, feeling hopeful for the first time in months.

The next day, I drove straight through to the salon where she worked. We had a cordial, light greeting and agreed to meet back at home later to talk. I drove home and waited anxiously until her shift ended. When she arrived home, we were polite and careful in our words. I made my case for a separation, citing all the reasons the trip had been beneficial and how we were only spinning our wheels and keeping up appearances by remaining together at this point. She listened attentively and at length and when I was finished, she sat silently.

After a minute, she told me she was pregnant. She wasn't sure, she said, if it were mine or Victor's. I sat reeling. I did not know if this was the happiest news or the worst tragedy or some combination of the two rolled into one. She took out her planner and flipped back a page and began to explain how it made more sense that the baby was Victor's. Judging from the calendar, it would have had to have been a minor miracle for me to have had much to do with it, incapacitated and comatose on the sofa in my depression. She told me that when informed of the pregnancy, Victor had wanted nothing to do with it. I now had to ask myself some very difficult questions.

I had taken my vows before God, my family, and my friends in a second wedding ceremony where we had been married by the Monsignor, and I took my vows gravely and seriously. But above all, it was my own experience of my parents' divorce that informed my decision. I simply could not walk out on my wife the way my father had walked out on my mother. It was a matter of principle to me and I chose to stay, for better or worse, as I had vowed. I also knew there was no way that Cynthia could raise the child alone and there was a young life to be considered here, regardless of paternity. I simply could not turn my back on a child in need. I chose to assume the role of father, regardless of paternity, knowing that I would automatically go down on the birth certificate as the father of any child born during our marriage.

And so I called off my plans for a trial separation and prepared instead for new fatherhood.

Given the fact that I would be the legal father and that of Victor's disinterest, I decided to forego a paternity test. Besides, it made no difference now that I had chosen to accept and love the child as my own regardless. It was irrelevant and a moot point. If anyone had questions at the birth, well, it was none of their business and hopefully no one would be so insensitive as to point out the potential disparity of a Scandinavian father and a brown-skinned child.

I adored fatherhood. Brandon was the most beautiful thing on Earth and the easiest baby. He never fussed and we took him everywhere, even to the movie theater starting at a month old where he slept through an action film. Brandon had the sweetest, most joyful disposition, always laughing and giggling. His bright blue eyes, round cheeks, and wispy light brown hair were angelic. I loved nothing more than dressing him in cute little outfits and my store discount at the Broadway made that endless fun. We shared many special moments together, father and son hiking in the Santa Susana mountains with Brandon in a carrier on my back. Cynthia would bring him to the store where he was such a delight and a huge hit in the Men's Department which I was now running, having recently been promoted to Department Manager. I had a beautiful new family and a new promotion, and life was great.

It seemed, however, that around a year into our domestic bliss, Cynthia grew restless once more. She wanted to be out with her friends again and I readily agreed to stay home with Brandon so she could do so. I loved watching SpongeBob and doing bath time and bedtime stories. But this time, when Cynthia stayed out longer or gave me a little more than a wave of the hand during her less frequent pit stops, I was not so understanding.

Also, I still had my own desires and curiosities that I had set aside for the sake of the marriage and for fatherhood. Those desires had not subsided any and I was resentful at putting myself on the shelf only to feel used and burned up each night. Of course, I never discussed this with Cynthia and in all fairness, things may have played out differently if I had summoned the courage to speak my truth. Instead, I sat in my resentment until it became unbearable. I asked a high school friend if I could stay with him, and told Cynthia I wanted a separation after all.

CHAPTER 4

A few months earlier, I waited on an intriguing gentleman in my Men's Department. Kent was in his early forties, attractive, and lively with bright blue eyes and a sly smile. He flirted with me shamelessly while I helped him select a wardrobe for a trip to Italy. I very much enjoyed his attention and asked him to stop by and say hello upon his return. And now, he was idling alongside me in his 4Runner as I walked along the side of the road. He invited me back to his place for a drink.

My pulse quickened and I swung the door open and jumped in eagerly. As he pulled into traffic, I stole a glance at his profile. He was breathtaking. He exuded easy masculinity. Sandy brown hair fell rakishly into his eyes and his jawline was rugged and strong. His brawny chest heaved against his light blue t-shirt and hinted of understated virility. Long, elegant fingers wrapped around the wheel lightly as he handled it effortlessly. We chatted casually, getting reacquainted as we drove.

We pulled into the garage of a well-manicured tract home and he closed the garage door behind us, then took my hand and I followed him inside. He led me from room to room, passing through hallways lined with dozens of artful, expertly framed photographs he had taken around the world. An immaculate baby grand piano sat center stage in a formal living room.

He led me into the bedroom and as we undressed I regarded his lean, tan frame and soon, we fell into leisurely and languid lovemaking. He held my gaze and encouraged me to be selfish and indulgent with his generosity; only now, there was none of the fear or dread that eye contact had brought before. Rather, his gaze spurred me on to greater heights and mischievous play. This was entirely new. And in between takes, I rested on his strong, broad chest as we talked and laughed as he tousled my hair.

And when it was over and we lay spent and I knew it was time to go, he asked if I wanted to grab some dinner, then come back and do it all again.

The next morning, after a sumptuous meal of eggs benedict, Bloody Marys, and another round of luxurious lovemaking, he drove me by my friend's apartment where I picked up my belongings and I moved into the beautiful house with the grand piano and the vintage French books and the artful and evocative black and white photography…and never looked back.

Ours was a very boozy affair. We were not drinking alcoholically, but we were definitely drinking lavishly. I quickly learned that there was a drink for every occasion. I was also learning that everything was better with booze. At last, I was learning to unwind. By that second cocktail in the den after work, the stress of the day seemed to melt away and I could move on to the next exciting phase of the evening with my beautiful and adventurous, virile boyfriend as we'd head out to make the town our playground.

Most of all, I was loving the sexual inhibition alcohol delivered. Under Kent's gentle tutelage and encouragement, I was coming into my own at last, shedding the self-consciousness that had made sex with other men awkward and fraught with shame. With the right amount of liquid courage, I could really let myself fly free and reach new heights of confidence and daring. It was decadent and delicious and terribly indulgent. And it was mine, every night.

When I told Cynthia I had moved in with Kent and wanted to divorce, she exploded. She told me she would fight me and I would never see Brandon again. She outed me to my parents, to my employer, and to all of our friends. I was devastated.

In tears, I told Kent I couldn't take it anymore and I needed out of Thousand Oaks. He asked me where I wanted to go. I told him I had been thinking about applying with airlines again and he told me that if I got an offer and passed training, he would move with me. I was floored. He said he was ready for a new adventure, which I had brought into his life. I was so grateful to not only have found the love of my life, but someone who would support me in my own dreams, and I dove headlong into the application process, desperate to get us out of town.

Business Express was a major regional airline that operated out of New York and Boston. It was a perfect match as Kent's company was headquartered in nearby New Hampshire and a lateral transfer would be easy to arrange. Secondly, Business Express was one of the first airlines to offer travel privileges to unmarried domestic partners. And because the airline operated flights on behalf of both Delta and Northwest, they offered travel privileges with both major airlines which would facilitate my visitation with Brandon in California. I sent off my application and was hired at company headquarters a week later. Kent and I were both very excited about starting over in progressive Boston, with its grand architecture and cultural opportunities.

We met with a rental agent in Boston who showed us several properties, each more beautiful than the last. On the way back to the airport, our agent asked if we'd like to see one more listing that had just come available. We pulled up in front of a formidable, three-story brownstone at 38 The Fenway, next to the Boston Conservatory of Music and Berkeley College. A sweeping bay window overlooked a compact lawn shaded by a magnificent elm. It was a grand home. The house sat across the street facing the Back Bay Fens and the Victory Gardens and a jewel-like waterway that lazed through a grove of gracious weeping willows. Our agent checked his listing again to be certain that this was the right building, as this appeared to be far too commanding a space for our budget. We walked up the three marble steps onto the stoop, swung the door open, and stepped into a marble-floored landing beneath an ornate wrought iron chandelier. A second door led to three more steps and an expansive oak-floored, high ceilinged foyer with a floor-to-ceiling fireplace on one side and a sweeping grand stairway on the other. Wainscoting surrounded the room and sconces lit the space cheerfully.

The home was breathtaking in its grandeur. We stared at one another, certain there had been some mistake. We pressed on into a long and formal dining room with two brass chandeliers descending from the 15-foot ceiling and another floor-to-ceiling fireplace. A cut-glass skylight radiated down the softest light from above the three-story grand staircase bathing the home in a pale, warm glow. In all, the home was 2,500 square feet of coal pantries, maids' quarters, secret passageways, and stables. It was a home filled with mystery and intrigue which captured the imagination and would not let go. We said goodbye to the magical home, hurried off to Logan, and boarded our DC-10 flight back to Los Angeles, our heads swimming.

Kent and I both tried to put the unlikely and impractical mansion out of our minds on the long flight home. Midway across the country, I saw that Kent was sketching the floor plan of the brownstone on a pad of graph paper in the darkened cabin. He was planning where to put the furniture and making a list of the necessary repairs it would take to make the home a showplace. I knew he was as excited as I was by the endless possibilities of the home. I leaned over his shoulder and watched him work as he sketched artfully and urgently, his sleeves rolled back and his forearms taught. Suddenly, he drew a box beneath the floorplan and wrote in it:

Kent Heckart and Steven Slater
38 The Fenway
Boston, MA

I smiled and buried my face in his shoulder. We had truly found a home of our own.

Boston was magical. We arrived at holiday time and took a penthouse at the corner of Beacon and Massachusetts Avenue while we waited for the paperwork and repairs on the brownstone to be completed. 438 Beacon had a wraparound terrace at the top of the building which gave us a 360-degree views of the city below. We set out at once to explore Back Bay's cultural and culinary delights. I joined the Boston of Museum of Fine Arts and began attending lectures at the nearby Isabella Stewart Gardner Museum on my days off while Kent was away working at his office in New Hampshire. I loved being back in the sky and was in my element once more. My trips took me all around New England, into Canada, and in and out of New York City daily.

It was not long before we moved into the brownstone and as expected, it needed work. Since I was home on call with the airline while Kent was at his office all day, much of it fell to me. While the house was architecturally stunning, it had fallen into some disrepair and disregard over the years. I was adamant it should be restored to its original grandeur in short order. However, having never undertaken such a project, I had no idea what such efforts entailed.

The first restoration project I set my eyes on was the rehabilitation of the grand staircase. As the staircase was the most prominent and noteworthy architectural feature of the home, I believed this the most logical place to begin my efforts. Ornate and sweeping, the staircase ascended three stories in wainscoted grandeur. Brass sconces jutted from the wall lighting the way and a threadbare oriental runner ran the length of the stairwell down the center.

I saw Kent off to work one morning then set off for the hardware store where I bought sandpaper, steel wool, stripper, and turpentine. Returning to the house, I set to work. With coarse grain sandpaper, I began sanding the first step on the landing in the main foyer. One hundred years of stain and finish refused to budge. Frustrated, I switched to steel wool which only kicked up a light dusting. Clearly, I was not going to be able to do this by hand. I poured a healthy coating of finish remover and turpentine on to the steps and let it sit while I redirected my efforts towards hacking at the runner with a knife and a pair of scissors, yet I could not get the fabric to budge from the staircase. I began to scrub wildly at the turpentine and stripper with the steel wool but all that came off was a gelatinous blob of remover with shards of splintered, ancient wood which became embedded in the steel wool pad and pierced the palms of my hand as I scrubbed desperately.

This was nothing like what I had in mind and I became enraged, yelling obscenities that reverberated off the skylight above and back down the stairwell. Incensed, I began stabbing the runner with the knife until it impaled in the wood and got stuck.

When Kent came home many hours later, he found me on my knees on the staircase, my hands raw and bloodied. He was horrified. He asked what I was doing and I wailed at him, "What the fuck does it look like I am doing?" I launched into a barely coherent diatribe about the house and my need to have it perfect at that moment. In reality, I had flipped into a manic episode, the first he had witnessed from me, and lost my wits.

This became a frightening pattern, as my bipolar mania manifested itself. Each day, Kent would leave for work, and I would begin my full-fledged assault on the house. Within hours, I would be bloodied and battered, screaming and yelling in a masochistic, one-man war on the stoic, hundred-year-old mansion. Kent would come home to find me in exactly the same place he had left me, beyond reason, and another fight would ensue.

Before this point, I had only known the sadness and crushing sorrow of bipolar depression. But now the pendulum had swung the other way and I was in full-fledged mania, unable to control my impulses and desires. To make things worse, in my irrational state I could not understand why Kent did not have his sleeves rolled up working alongside me. I accused him of being disinterested and not carrying his part of the deal, when in fact he was simply trying to keep us fed and mentally intact. Many nights, he would throw his hands up in frustration and head to bed, only to creep out of the bedroom at 3 or 4 in the morning to find me ensconced on the stairwell scrubbing away like some Phantom of the Staircase.

Bipolar had come calling, only we didn't know what to call it. All either of us knew was that I was making things unbearable for both of us and jeopardizing our beautiful new start together in our new home.

I transferred to the newly-opened Buffalo base where I was number one in seniority. In California, Kent and I had enjoyed a robust sex life. We were hot and heavy, always at the ready. But now in Boston, it was different. Kent was now commuting two hours each way to New Hampshire to work and I was often exhausted from a two-leg commute to Buffalo. It was getting harder to coordinate quality time to enjoy together. Kent was also becoming resentful of my time away, and my crazy crew of young friends in Buffalo who were getting more and more of my time and energy each week. While Kent was at the office each day, I was free to flit about the city, sometimes for days on end, with no obligations. I was twenty-three, newly out, and just liberated from a disastrous marriage. I had much lost time to make up for. Walking around the city each day, I met many intriguing men and I attracted attention as any twenty-three-year-old gay boy would.

Because I did not know about bipolar, I did not know about hypersexuality, a symptom of bipolar that creates an insatiable drive and had been the source of such angst my teen years. Everywhere I looked in the cosmopolitan and progressive city, I saw young, gay men living out loud and I wanted to be a part of that scene at last. I loved Kent endlessly, but I was young and restless. I knew sex lay just outside my reach in the park across the street, and in the leather bar called the Ramrod up on the corner.

I listened with shut eyes as Kent backed out of the driveway then pulled up the alley and onto Boylston. I descended the half-finished staircase and walked into the kitchen. *How could I even consider cheating on such a good man?* I scolded inwardly, ashamed. I knew I did not have it in me. Then it occurred to me. A drink might help me find the courage. I reached under the kitchen cabinet and pulled out of a fifth of vodka. I poured myself a glass, 3/4 full. I topped it off with a little bit of orange juice and slammed it down. I hadn't even made my morning coffee yet. Shortly, a familiar warmth radiated through my body and I began to feel more confident and at ease. A second screwdriver went down easier, and before long, I was feeling strong and sassy. In that moment, I knew

I had crossed a line. I knew that alcohol could do for me what I could not do for myself. I was aware that I was drinking purely for effect. I told myself I would think about that when I came back home later.

Within minutes, I was lost on a tide of orgiastic pleasure as I floated across the city from one partner to the next. Kent was already home when I finally slunk back in the door, chastened and sober, and confessed what I had done, unable to reconcile my dishonesty. Kent was kind and compassionate but adamant that this was not a road he was willing to trudge in his life. To end our relationship on a high note, we dressed in our finest and went to the Capital Grille. We ordered Chateaubriand for two and a bottle of Dom Perignon and toasted the highlights of our beautiful life together. When we returned to the brownstone, we made love. The next morning, Kent drove me to the airport where he handed me a red rose and saw me off on the morning flight to Buffalo.

CHAPTER 5

The 747 felt sure and solid as I surveyed the cabin from my oversized sleeper seat in Trans World One. The cabin was situated in the nose of the aircraft, the spiral staircase to my left ascending to the flight deck above. Wine bottles and crystal stemware reflected soft, diffused lighting and the occasional plink of silver flatware against fine china lent an air of opulence and refinement to the surroundings.

It was the summer of 1996 and I was a new hire Trans World Airlines flight attendant enjoying the travel privileges that came with working for a major international airline.

I had been visiting Kent, who remained a dear friend, at the brownstone on a Boston layover when I spotted an ad in the Boston Globe. TWA was hiring flight attendants and hosting an open house downtown. Flying for Trans World Airlines had long seemed an impossible dream. Business Express and TWA shared a terminal at Logan and I would stare with barely concealed envy as the glamorous and worldly TWA flight attendants glided down the concourse in their timeless and classic Ralph Lauren uniforms, wearing shoes from Rome and gold jewelry from Cairo. TWA's Flight 810 left for Paris at 8 o'clock each night and I would look up from the frozen tarmac at the sleek white 767 adorned with two red stripes and the letters "TWA" illuminated high upon the tail. As I shivered and froze on the stairs of my tiny commuter plane, I would see the ethereal flight attendants hanging coats and floating through the aisles with trays of champagne. But I never dreamed that one day I could float down that aisle myself. Besides, TWA rarely hired flight attendants. Certainly, everyone would be clamoring at this opportunity. I wouldn't stand a chance.

I finished my trip in Buffalo and jumped on the first flight back to Boston to attend the open house. About twenty-five candidates assembled in a meeting room where we were greeted warmly by four poised TWA flight attendants. We were then each given an opportunity to come to the front of the room and introduce ourselves, then to field a series of questions thrown at us by the interviewers. I was asked what book was on my bedside table, how I motivated myself to excellence, what was my favorite quote, and what I might say to a passenger whose Louis Vuitton garment bag had been torn in the coat closet of a 727. We were asked if we spoke a foreign language and if so, to speak a few words. My Spanish classes in high school had finally paid off.

At the end of the interview, we were each handed an envelope with TWA's red and white logo in the upper corner. It would contain a letter either thanking us for our time or inviting us to a second interview at company headquarters in St Louis. I snatched up my envelope and ran to the lobby as discreetly as possible. Throwing myself down in a wingback chair, I tore into my envelope and quickly scanned the letter. I had been invited for the second interview.

At the training center, we were put in a 747 cabin simulator and asked to operate emergency and service equipment, make public announcements, and push meal and beverage carts through the aisles. I had a great rapport with my interviewer, a senior, male purser who had served aboard everything from the 707 to the 747 and who I found fascinating yet relatable.

Of all the airlines I've trained with, TWA best prepared us for the rigors of the job. Because Trans World Airlines was an international flag carrier, TWA aircraft were often the target of terrorism. For this reason, TWA security training was the best in class. We took numerous courses on aviation security, learning to identify various assault weapons that had been used in attacks on our aircraft.

The most hair-raising training drill I ever participated in occurred the night we were put in a 727 cabin simulator and told we would be practicing meal services. We were comfortably seated in the passenger cabin while two flight attendant trainees simulated serving out of the forward galley and two more worked from a galley in the rear. An alarm sounded, indicating a fire in an aft lavatory. The two trainee flight attendants in the aft began fighting the fire when suddenly, two men portraying hijackers ran up the aisles shouting obscenities and brandishing rifles. They demanded entrance into the cockpit and then at once, there was the sound of gunfire followed by a loud bang and a flash, then everything went dark.

The cabin trainer jerked and lurched then dropped out from under us and came to rest at a 45 degree angle as alarms began to sound. The captain's voice came over the P.A. system with the order to evacuate. The flight attendants began calling us forward to the exits, only to find that the instructors had jammed them remotely. We were on our hands and knees following the aisle emergency lighting in pitch blackness when one quick-thinking trainee remembered that we had been shown how to use the cockpit window as a last-ditch escape path earlier in the day. This was what the instructors had been waiting for. All twenty-four of us had to climb out the cockpit window and drop to the ground below and roll away from the simulator.

In all, it took us over two minutes to evacuate the trainer. In our post-drill debriefing, we were reminded that in an actual emergency, we would have had less than 90 seconds to evacuate a full aircraft of 146 passengers before toxic fumes and flames would have overtaken the cabin. I went back to my hotel room that night shaken, with a new appreciation for my airline, and the gravity of my new responsibilities. TWA did not play.

Based in New York City, my training class was fortunate to come online during a major expansion of TWA's flight schedule and I held a regular set schedule upon graduation, flying aboard the DC-9 each week with layovers in Dallas/Ft. Worth, Minneapolis, and Milwaukee.

I joined five of my classmates in a townhouse apartment in Kew

Gardens, close enough to both JFK and LaGuardia Airports to be convenient for work and just a train ride away from the city. The neighborhood contained several fun bars and pubs frequented by airline crew and there was always something going on at all hours. On my days off, I jumped on the Long Island Railroad and explored Manhattan.

To celebrate my new chapter, I picked up my first international trip, Flight 810 to Paris, the flight I so enviously watched set sail for Paris from the steps of my little regional plane so many times. I flew up to Boston the night before and Kent threw a Bon Voyage party with all our friends.

I worked First Class on that trip and never felt more glamorous or beautiful as I did in the aisle of the elegant 767, pouring champagne and serving escargot and foie gras to my refined American and French guests who each boarded with a valise, a hardcover book, and an appetite for airborne adventure.

I was now part of a TWA legacy that included Charles Lindbergh and Howard Hughes and set the hallmark for international travel and style. TWA was the Airline of Stars. Indeed, Elizabeth Taylor and Richard Burton flew TWA, booking the entire First Class cabin for themselves. Pope John Paul often said the letters "TWA" stood for Traveling With Angels. My life was never so beautiful as it was high above the North Atlantic that day.

At 8:02 p.m. on July 17, 1996, TWA Flight 800, a Boeing 747, pushed back from gate 27 at the TWA Flight Center at New York's John F. Kennedy International Airport, destined for Paris' Charles de Gaulle Airport and Rome Fiumicino. At 8:19 p.m. the majestic red and white airliner lifted gracefully into the twilight of the warm summer night and made a gentle, sweeping turn out over the Atlantic, beginning what was to have been her long overnight crossing. At 8:31 p.m., nearly the exact same moment the sun hid its last light behind the horizon, an explosion of controversial origin brought the 747 and all those aboard down into the sea approximately seven miles east of Fire Island.

Half a world away, blissfully unaware of the horrors that had befallen what was to have been our inbound aircraft for our return flight to New York in the morning, my crew and I were resting peacefully on the second of two beautiful nights in the Eternal City enjoying one of the most coveted layovers in the TWA system. I had gotten the call for the trip from crew scheduling just before my reserve duty ended two days earlier. And so it came to be that I found myself ensconced with wide-eyed wonder in the city that quickly captured my heart and holds it tightly to this day.

On the morning of July 18th, I awoke lazily to enjoy some fresh bread and prosciutto I had purchased the night before. Suddenly, there was a furious pounding on the wall from the room next door. I threw on a shirt and looked into the hallway to see that my flying partner's door was open. He motioned me in, his face ashen as he sat glued to the television, mesmerized. The image on the screen was one of blackness dotted with occasional orange flames. Within a few seconds of glancing at the image, the phone rang, and my friend answered the call from the front desk informing us that our flight was "indefinitely delayed." Hanging up the phone, he relayed the mystifying conversation to me, and I put together a scenario which I thought made perfect sense.

In 1988, I had been booked on a Pan Am flight from New York to Rome that had been cancelled when Mediterranean airspace had been closed due to the U.S. bombing of Libya. Certainly the images we were seeing must have been of oil fields burning in the night, images made familiar during the Gulf War. Clearly, we must have gone back into Libya overnight and were now unable to overfly the area as had been the case in years past. "Oh," I said with a sigh of relief, "it's just more Desert Storm. We'll be stuck here for a while," I declared, feeling worldly and wise. "We may as well just head down and get a cappuccino," I said, feeling somewhat excited by the prospect of another day in this beautiful city and in no hurry to get back to the Q10 bus and an apartment shared with five other new hires in New York.

"No. That's not it at all," my friend said, his eyes wide. "Look!" he exclaimed, as the words "TWA 800" rolled across the bottom of the screen. My stomach lurched and a roar rushed through my temples. My head spun in confusion as I tried to figure out what this all meant.

"Timetable!" we both screamed out nearly in unison as he began rummaging wildly through his tote bag looking for a schedule. He then began tearing through a dog-eared copy he found inside, a Summer 1996 System Timetable with a painting of a Constellation and a 747 on the cover, the words "Celebrating 50 years of Transatlantic Service" proudly splashed across the cover. "Paris!" he shouted out next and a heavy sorrow descended upon the room in the heavy silence that followed as the implication of this information became clear: a 747, lots of fuel, a big crew, and a heavy passenger load.

After a moment, we began discussing our own dilemma. This news was terrible, but we couldn't quite connect how this tragedy off the coast of New York was the cause of our "indefinite delay" out of Rome. We were to operate Flight 849, which flew Rome-New York-Los Angeles. We sat in his room for about an hour, glued to the television and awaiting further word from operations when finally a note was slid under the door informing us of a crew gathering in one of the hotel's function rooms in about an hour.

Shell-shocked, I returned to my room and finished dressing, then proceeded down the hall shortly where I joined the two other 747 crews who were staying in the hotel. Word of the crash had spread quickly through the hallways and now some forty TWA pilots and flight attendants had come together to seek and exchange information, to comfort and console one another, and in many instances, to begin the process of mourning those lost.

It was here, in this expansive meeting room, that the agonizing answers to our many questions were revealed, and where we came to learn of the perfect storm that had caused our flight out of Rome to be cancelled forever that morning.

On the night of July 17th, a mechanical problem had grounded TWA Flight 848, the second of TWA's twice-daily 747 flights to Rome, causing it to be combined with Flight 800 to Paris. Thus came to be the unique routing of flight 800's New York-Paris-Rome journey instead of two separate non-stop flights to Europe. This now meant that the crew originally designated to operate the Rome flight would now deadhead, or ride as passengers on the Paris sector and then continue on to Rome as working crew, so Flight 800 now carried on board a total of 35 JFK-based pilots and flight attendants instead of the standard crew of 17. To further compound the tragedy, TWA's Flight 810, which operated between Boston and Paris, had been cancelled that night as well and the Boston passengers had been routed through JFK to travel aboard Flight 800.

We sat in a wide circle now, myself and nearly forty of my grief-stricken colleagues in various states of shock, and passed a copy of the flight manifest around the circle. Watching the hearts of my colleagues shatter as their tear-filled eyes scanned the list and landed on the names of lifelong friends was agonizing and I had to look away often as I sat in dread, knowing I would most likely recognize a name or two myself once I took the list into my own hands.

Tears slipped from my eyes as I read the name of flight engineer Richard Campbell and remembered him laughing heartily down from the spiral staircase as I stood below in the First Class galley on a recent trip. I could feel twenty-four-year-old Jill Ziemkiewicz's radiance as she described the beautiful gown she had found for her upcoming wedding as we walked in stride pulling our wheeled suitcases down the concourses in St. Louis just a few weeks earlier, and I could see Flight Service Manager Lani Warren standing regally at the boarding door in her timeless Ralph Lauren uniform welcoming me aboard proudly as I boarded the 767 that took me back to Boston and Kent the day I was hired with TWA in St. Louis. After the service, Lani had come back and sat with us excited new hires and shared her story of her treasured career that spanned decades.

As I began to shudder reading the list, a strong and solid arm reached out and around me seemingly from nowhere, and a 747 captain I had not met before pulled me close. We spoke privately off to the side and I shared my story of SkyWest Flight 5569. He told me that I had seen far too much loss for my young age but cautioned me that I would probably see more if I stayed in the business. He took me under his wing for the rest of the morning, lending me some much needed fatherly strength.

Before long, the mourning turned toward celebration and we all started to share stories and remembrances of our friends. Small, informal groups broke off and eventually, laughter began to ease the pain a bit and I got the privilege of watching my TWA family do what they did best: love one another.

Yet I felt that as a new hire, half the age of most of my colleagues, I had no place among professionals who had just lost loved ones of twenty or thirty years and so I tried to sneak back to my room. Feeling ashamed and something of an accidental voyeur, I discreetly excused myself from the room and headed down the hallway and the privacy of my room. A senior flight attendant named Pat saw me make my clandestine move for the elevator and knowingly intercepted me and would not allow me to run from the moment. She gently guided me around me around a corner to a quiet spot and we had a beautiful and loving talk that changed everything.

Pat told me that we were one TWA family and reminded me that this loss affected us all no matter how long we had served. She said that certainly our beloved airline would never be the same again and no one knew what the future would bring. She told me that this loss would affect us all deeply, yet differently, so to expect many different reactions and to take nothing personally. And then another senior flight attendant joined us and hugged me tearfully, wanting to know how I was doing. Here were these beautiful and elegant senior flight attendants who had just lost lifelong friends reaching out to me, a new hire reserve, to nurture and soothe my pain, and soon I found that I was able to do the same in kind for others. These wonderful ladies taught me that when we give of ourselves to care for another, the more profound the healing we experience for ourselves. Today, I no longer shy away from someone's pain, but rather offer to sit alongside them in it. When we sit quietly and hold a hand, our hand is held as well. And when we love another wholeheartedly, we love our own hearts back to wholeness.

After some time, a few of us wandered down to the hotel restaurant and had a somber meal together. I had little appetite and only nibbled on some hard rolls but the company did me good.

Afterwards, I found myself needing a more profound sustenance. Only a higher power could provide comfort in the midst of such a storm, and I longed for a place of spiritual refuge. A quick walk through the lobby and hallways turned up a few others who felt the same. I remembered that Pope John Paul II had long traveled on TWA aircraft and had called TWA "Traveling With Angels." Five of us headed out for the Vatican. At the entrance to the walled city, we simply flashed our yellow and red TWA ID badges to the guard whose face immediately softened into a look of compassionate understanding and we were immediately shepherded inside the museum. We wandered through the beautiful artifacts of the Vatican Museum collection which provided a welcome distraction, but it was the Sistine Chapel that beckoned ahead, promising solace and serenity from the sorrow of the last several hours.

As one enters the Sistine Chapel, the silence is both enveloping and insular and the serenity quiets the soul. It is as if time ceases to exist and one senses an eternal, impermeable stillness. It was, as hoped, the one place I felt out of sorrow's reach, if only for a moment. There, I lifted my heart in prayer for my colleagues and their passengers lost at sea, for my brokenhearted coworkers, and my company which now faced unprecedented challenges.

Back at the hotel, I realized I had better call my mom in California. She answered on the first ring and let out a sob when she heard my voice. She then relayed the story of how she had driven up the coast with a friend on the night of the 16th and missed my message about lucking out with a trip to Rome. Her answering machine was an antiquated number that did not timestamp messages. She had come home on the 17th and listened to my message in which I said I was leaving for Rome and then turned on the television only to see the remains of a TWA aircraft, destined for Paris and Rome in flames on the ocean's surface. Numerous attempts to contact TWA had only met with jammed circuits and busy signals. Now, we hung on the line, neither of us able to speak, crying together and watching the news. My next call was to Kent in Boston, who had also been anxiously watching the news as well. He invited me to come to Boston straightaway upon my return to New York and I made plans to do just that.

When the first TWA aircraft arrived in Rome a day later, we boarded with great trepidation, not knowing what had brought the mighty and venerable 747 down to Earth two days earlier. Suspecting terrorism, we braced ourselves for any number of unpleasant scenarios on our return flight to JFK. Yet we steeled ourselves not only because we had a job to do in honor of our fallen colleagues, but because on board with us were several family members of those lost in the crash. One such passenger was an elderly Italian grandmother who had lost both her daughter and granddaughter in the crash. Seeing me struggle with my own emotions and shaking as I tried to pour coffee in the aisle, she rose from her seat and wrapped her arms around me. She stroked my hair and whispered words of comfort in Italian as we just stood there in the aisle comforting one another.

Arrival in New York was both somber and celebratory. We were met by both the base manager and our union representatives who escorted us to Hanger 12 where we received a tear-filled, hearty welcome from everyone we came across. The sight of Air Force One parked inside the hanger and black- clad snipers positioned on the roof and scattered throughout the employee parking lot, however, was not lost on any of us and ratcheted up the already high anxiety to even loftier levels.

The resplendent red and white colors of our glorious TWA no longer grace the skies, but who will ever forget where they were the night of July 17, 1996, the night which drew an indelible mark in time and resoundingly delineated an idyllic before and an irreversible, sorrowful after from which there could be no return? What we woke up to in Rome and around the TWA system was unprecedented and incomprehensible. Yet that morning crews the world over donned their navy uniforms and rose to the challenge of delivering the gold standard of service and unparalleled safety even as we grappled with staggering personal loss that took our breath away. Despite the uncertainty and confusion of those first harrowing days, the people of TWA held their heads high and performed their jobs with admirable professionalism that became the envy of an industry the world over. Our loyal and esteemed passengers came aboard expressing their continued confidence in our company, our maintenance, and our crews. We worked diligently to show our gratitude and to prove to the world that its trust was well placed. We did it with a sense of renewed pride that morning and in the days to come, for we did it in honor of our dear departed colleagues, the crew of TWA Flight 800, forever in our hearts. The true legacy of TWA.

I connected to the last flight from JFK to Boston and collapsed into a seat in first class. Kent was waiting for me at the top of the jetway in Boston, a single red rose in hand just as he had seen me off to Buffalo a few months earlier. I crumpled into his arms and began to sob as the tension, stress, and trauma of the last 48 hours overwhelmed me as the stream of passengers coming up the jetway and those moving along the concourse regarded the scene compassionately and parted, stepping delicately around us with care. By now the whole world had heard the news of the disaster and it was clear to all who passed that I was somehow personally linked to the tragedy.

Kent drove me home and warmed up some soup while I showered. He listened as I talked long into the night trying to gather my racing thoughts. Finally, both too exhausted to continue, he wrapped me in his arms and gently laid me on his bed, then laid down beside me and pulled me close, holding me tightly.

The next thing I knew, I was screaming and clawing at the darkness as images of my friends falling through the night sky replayed in my mind. A massive explosion had broken the aircraft into two parts, spilling its occupants into the ocean below. This horrific image had been seared into my brain by the repetitive news reports and I watched obsessively. I had been unable to come to terms with it in my waking hours. Now it was positively overwhelming my weary and exhausted psyche as I tried to sleep. Each time I would drift off, the gruesome, intrusive image would jar me back awake and I would lurch into panic and terror. Soon, it was intermingling with long-buried, horrific images from the SkyWest crash site until I was so strung out and angst-ridden that sleep was completely impossible. Each time I would fly upright in bed screaming, Kent would gently pull me back down and envelope me in his loving arms, rocking and soothing me back to sleep.

Back in New York a few days later, I was assigned a bittersweet flight on which I was proud to serve, an MD-80 flight from JFK to Denver and Salt Lake City carrying the human remains of four of Flight 800's victims, including one of our pilots. I was assigned the First Class cabin which was reserved solely for the family members escorting their loved ones below. The families were pre-boarded at JFK by TWA Care Team volunteers and we were introduced to one another before general boarding commenced.

We took off around sunset and headed west for Denver and as I served the first round of drinks, I found that most everyone was interested in circulating around the cabin and speaking with one another so we decided to hold off on dinner and just lounge around and visit for a while. The families got to know one another and shared stories about their loved ones. It was so lovely to be included in these conversations and to hear these beautiful memories. Everyone wanted to impress upon me how wonderful TWA and our volunteers had been to them despite the negative publicity the airline had received in the press. The criticism had been that the airline had been slow to release the passenger list but the truth was that the FBI had seized the manifest nearly immediately after the accident and the company was prohibited from commenting on it as the investigation unfolded.

It was a beautiful, clear night and we chased the sunset into the inky twilight and a deep, violet, night sky. As the night went on, I served dinner and kept the drinks flowing, and laughter and a few tears filled the forward cabin. Upon landing in Denver, however, things took a reverent tone and we bid a teary and formal farewell to our new family and handed them over to more TWA volunteers and a phalanx of ground staff who lined the jetway to pay their respects before we headed on to Salt Lake City where the scene was repeated. I found the honor of working this flight both life changing and humbling and I am forever grateful to have been a part of it.

The crash of Flight 800 took a heartrending toll on TWA and its loyal employees as we found ourselves in an unprecedented collective period of grief and mourning. In all, TWA lost 53 family members in the tragedy. With thirty-five crew members lost in the crash, nearly everyone at the JFK base had known someone aboard that flight. Prior to the accident, TWA was making a remarkable and resounding comeback. The company was profitable and expanding for the first time in years. We had just won a prestigious JD Power Award and were in the process of renewing the fleet with fuel efficient 717 and 757 aircraft.

Now overnight, our future appeared tenuous at best. The Lockheed L-1011 fleet was retired and plans were made to phase out the beloved 747 as well. This meant an immediate 25% reduction in flying from the JFK base and a furlough of a proportionate number of flight attendants. Crunching the numbers, it was hard to see how my exciting new job would be spared for more than a few months. I went back on reserve and found myself sitting at home for up to three weeks at a time without a flight assignment, which meant a huge financial strain.

CHAPTER 6

After not flying for a month, I was furloughed. About that time, a new, cute boy popped up in the neighborhood. His name was David, and he flew for Delta. David was a southern boy, hailing from the hills of Kentucky and I loved his cute accent and genteel manners. We started dating, and he suggested that I apply with Delta. Delta was hiring a lot of flight attendants and sending most everybody to New York. *Perfect*, I thought. I quickly sent off an application and was off to training with Delta in no time.

Upon graduation, I was assigned Cincinnati as my base and David transferred to join me. We found a gorgeous apartment on a rolling hillside overlooking a river in Northern Kentucky, and settled in quickly.

Unlike TWA with its long-haul transatlantic crossings, I was now flying short hops around the South in and out of Dallas/Ft. Worth and Atlanta. The pace was grueling, with most trips taking off before sunrise, but the Delta crews were welcoming and gracious, and I was just happy to be flying again.

In the midst of such bliss, however, I could never have known when I boarded Flight 1088, an MD-88 in Chicago heading home to Cincinnati on a late summer's afternoon in 1997, that my life would never be the same.

I had very much enjoyed working with my competent and

hospitable crew for the last three days. Brent, a year my senior, was the number one flight attendant. Handsome and professional, Brent set a welcoming tone in the First Class cabin and was a competent and confident purser. In the back, I worked well with a perky and hardworking new hire named Penny. I was thankful we only carried 80 people when the door was closed for departure. Among the passengers boarding in Chicago were three off-duty Delta flight attendants commuting to Cincinnati to work the London flight a few hours later. These ladies sat in my section of three rows behind the coach galley, a section which had no view of the outside as it was flanked by two jet engines on either side of the fuselage.

The aircraft pushed back from the gate on time around three in the afternoon and we ran through the safety demonstration in the aisle as the aircraft taxied to the end of the runway. I took my seat on the fold down jumpseat on the wall between the two rear-most toilets at the back of the aircraft, and Penny took her seat on the aisle of row 27, four rows forward of me, just in front of the galley on the left side of the aircraft.

I heard the thrust of the engines and felt the familiar forward surge of the aircraft as we started down the runway and soon we were catapulted forward and up into the air, climbing away from the airfield and out over Lake Michigan, on a direct course toward Cincinnati and home. At 10,000 feet, the captain called back on the interphone. Brent, Penny, and I picked up at once. The captain advised us to remain seated for a few minutes longer as there was "a little rough air" ahead. We all acknowledged and hung up. I felt slightly annoyed by the news, knowing we would have to work that much faster given the already short flight plan.

Within minutes, we started to experience the light chop, as promised. The aircraft bumped and swayed as if on a dirt road but nothing too alarming. The turbulence began to increase quite a bit and I shifted slightly in my jumpseat and tightened my harness, still not expecting anything too profound.

Suddenly, there was a sound akin to an explosion. A chorus of screams echoed throughout the cabin. The cabin floor was now rocketing up and down with such severe force and raw power that I could no longer see the front of the airplane. My head was whipped about badly and I couldn't see straight. This was nothing I had ever experienced before, and I knew this was a category of turbulence I had only read about in training and accident reports. We were in big trouble here.

The engines on either side of me began screaming in a metallic cacophony of screeching metal as suddenly exploded the deafening roar of a million hailstones slamming against the jet's aluminum skin at several hundred miles per hour, ricocheting off the rooftop and plinking against the glass windows with shotgun force. Suddenly, as if riding a giant carnival ride, there was a swirling, undulating motion as the back end of the aircraft begin to corkscrew in a sickening and nauseating flail as the tail end was lifted up and dropped down 50 to 100 feet at a time in a circular motion.

The left engine now wailed a sickening groan and began emitting a vibration which could be felt in my bones and made my teeth chatter. The commuting flight attendant two rows ahead of me looked towards the engine wide-eyed then spun around and looked at me and screamed over the deafening din, "Call the cockpit!" Certain the engine was about to rip from the fuselage, I reached for the intercom but the turbulence was too severe to grasp the handset.

Brent came over the PA, his voice shaking, instructing the passengers to check their seat belts and remain seated. He tried to remain composed but I could hear fear as his voice cracked. He repeated his instructions several times, then clicked off.

The jolts were so severe now, that the airframe made groaning, metallic, grinding sounds as the wings bowed up towards the top of the fuselage. Penny leaned forward and looked out the window at the wings folding up, then looked back at me. Our eyes locked. She was trembling. The intensity and the frequency of the jolts increased. Where it had felt as though we were slamming against a brick wall every few seconds now it was as if we were in a blender on puree.

Suddenly, the thought occurred to me, there is no way this airframe can withstand this. I thought calmly and clearly, *This airplane is going to break apart and I'm going to fall to my death. I'm going to know what it was like for my friends on Flight 800.* With that matter-of-fact statement came an enormous wash of sadness.

At once, everything went into slow motion. I looked around the airplane, at my terrified passengers, at Penny, at the debris in the aisle. I heard Brent's muffled and disembodied voice somewhere off in the distance as if through cotton wool. And in that moment, I accepted death. I reached my right hand out and gripped the lavatory door handle and with my left, I held onto my seat. I closed my eyes, and I simply waited for the moment. I prayed, and I asked God to take me quietly and quickly before the aircraft broke apart scattering me over the earth.

And then, there was the sound of an explosion. The engines screamed louder still and suddenly we were pitched violently up onto the right wing at a 90 degree angle and then, as if hit by a giant baseball bat, we were smashed severely back level with such force that I was pinned to my seat against the wall. I could not see out of the aircraft given my jumpseat position but everything had gone dark, almost black. In the next instant, the airplane was slammed violently up again onto the right wing and we were completely sideways but now, in the dark as well.

And then suddenly, another explosion deafened my ears in the darkened cabin and we were plunging, plummeting, not just dropping, but propelled downward at a sickening and nauseating speed that pinned me against the restraints of my jumpseat, unable to move. Down we plunged, thrust down a bottomless shaft with only Lake Michigan below to break our fall. Five seconds, six seconds, seven seconds, there was no end to the plummet and I knew we would only be stopped by the water's surface now, just like Flight 800. I closed my eyes and begged God to take me now. I was sick and bile rose to my throat and then the nose dropped and we were diving towards the lake and then somehow we were climbing and the engines were roaring mere feet away, louder than I had ever heard before. And the airplane shuddered and shook and the vibration jarred my brain as we bounced in a circle, fishtailing again. More screams from the cabin.

The airplane groaned and creaked and cracked and there was light again. I looked down. At my feet was a heavy green oxygen bottle. I got up and I stepped over the bottle and made my way to Penny's seat. Together, we looked out the window. We were soaring over calm, blue-green water, away from the angry gray sky that had beaten us like a child's toy. Brent made his way back from First Class and the three of us met in the middle of the cabin. We passed through the aisle together, checking for injuries and comforting our shell-shocked passengers.

Untrained on how to deal with the emotional aftermath of a near-death experience, we did what flight attendants the world over are trained to do. We put on our warmest smiles and went to work. We pretended everything was fine and we served complimentary cocktails like this was an everyday affair.

By the time I collected my luggage and hustled up the aisle at the gate in Cincinnati, the pilots were already on the way out the door and heading up the jetway. The captain was impatiently extricating himself from a shaken passenger. "Somewhere in excess of a thousand feet," he snapped, and hurried away up the jet bridge, without a backwards glance. I had many questions of my own about the hell I had just been put through and could have used a comforting word from our commander or at the very least, some answers. Just a few minutes earlier, I thought I was going to die over Lake Michigan. But apparently, this wasn't important enough to acknowledge. Therefore, it must not have been that big a deal. Clearly, Penny and Brent were shaken and we comforted one another. But in the end, I walked away from the airplane feeling guilty and embarrassed for my feelings. Ultimately, I felt abandoned.

Over the next few days, I waited to hear from my company. Certainly there would be many questions. I expected to be asked for a statement. Equally important, I knew my company would want to take care of me. We had a near-death experience. The crew was deeply traumatized.

After the crash of TWA Flight 800, TWA and my union orchestrated a mental health outreach for flight attendants that included access to therapists and mental health counselors on site. Upon return from Rome, I had met with a therapist in the flight attendant lounge and found it very helpful. Certainly, Delta understood the importance of Critical Incident Response and would be reaching out at any minute. But no such call ever came, and the incident went completely unacknowledged. I found this confusing and a bit infuriating as well. But mostly it underscored the misgivings I carried about my own feelings and mental health. Delta's indifference only served to validate my own shame and doubt, and caused me to second-guess what I thought I understood about my experience. If this experienced, professional organization didn't feel this event warranted concern, then perhaps it didn't.

In my personal life, I did not know how to approach the issue. David had been gracious and understanding but could not truly empathize with my story. My friends didn't seem to get it either. They would nod their heads understandingly and say how sorry they were, and then the conversation would go on without me while I stayed stuck behind. I felt the need to retell the tale time and again. Each time I did so, I relived it, which caused me to sink deeper into a dark place I could not return from. To make matters worse, David was flying a full schedule and I was often home alone at night when my symptoms were most acute.

The trauma of what I had just experienced on the Delta jet was now beginning to commingle with that left over from Flight 800 and SkyWest 5569 to create a complex PTSD that I was no match for. I knew nothing about PTSD, only that my life was becoming a living hell of anxiety, hypervigilance, and nightmares that was making every day a horror show.

I started to feel crippling anxiety before leaving for the airport for work. I could not bear to leave the apartment and the thought of a two- or three-day trip flooded me with cold dread. I was filled with separation anxiety and couldn't take the thought of being away from David. I was weepy and prone to crying jags, especially the closer I got to a flight. Once on board the aircraft, I felt overwhelmed and lost. I could barely breathe by the time the aircraft pushed back and I started having panic attacks on taxi as takeoff became inevitable. This was completely understandable for someone who had been through what I had endured, but I was too overwhelmed and frightened to ask for help.

Instead, I turned to alcohol. Alcohol was very effective in managing my symptoms, to a point. A bottle of wine in my hotel room at the end of the day could relax me enough that I could get to sleep and stay asleep without the ever-intrusive images of flailing bodies falling from the broken 747 disrupting my sleep once again.

Because I was so embarrassed by how high-strung and emotional I was around other people now, I made a point of pre-drinking before any social interaction, including spending time with David. This led to a lot of clandestine drinking. It meant I might have to have a couple on the way home from the airport, or make sure that I had a few before he made it home from work himself. If I were going to serve wine with dinner, I had to be sure I had a second bottle hidden in the kitchen to nip off of while I cooked.

All this added up to a great deal of booze. The acquisition and ingestion of so much sauce took a great deal of planning and execution, and soon became the central focus of my day.

Within a few months, I was stealing not only bottles of wine off the airplane to unwind at the end of a day of flying, but also a few vodka miniatures to get the next day started as well. A couple drinks in my hotel room in the morning would see me through security and onto the airplane, but one or two flights in, and my nerves would be shot and I would need more to keep me going so I began drinking on the airplane too, going to great lengths to hide my alcohol, only drinking vodka, and only stealing from First Class where the liquor wouldn't be missed. I was quickly losing control and careening into unmanageability.

On a thirty-six-hour Monroe, Louisiana, layover, I plugged the phone line into the dial-up modem of my laptop, and dialed long distance to New Orleans in search of a beau to help pass the time. Until then, I had been faithful, but I had already ingested a bottle of wine and 500 miles away from home, it seemed like a good idea at the time. I got into some heavy chatroom action over a second bottle of wine and promptly passed out over the keyboard. I awoke to the blaring alarm clock 24 hours later and in a panic, realized I had never disconnected the call. I raced downstairs to beat my crew to the front desk so no one would witness the spectacle about to unfold and was handed a bill for $535 in long-distance charges which I paid in my embarrassment and shame using my Delta Air Lines Credit Union debit card which was connected to the joint account I shared with David. David never mentioned the charge; either he never saw it or he chose his battles. Clearly, I was beginning to unravel.

For two nights, I tried to drink away the terror and anxiety that had ratcheted up to unmatched levels while David was away. I hadn't slept and I was so saturated I was unable to eat. I laid on a blanket on the floor listening to my European CDs for hours trying to make the room stop spinning. Finally, I decided on a drive hoping some fresh air might clear my head and settle my stomach. It was 2 a.m. when I staggered down the stairs and into David's Volvo, which I drove up the road with one eye closed, trying to keep it within the lines. I bought myself a 40 at the liquor store on the corner, then got back in the car, and set it between my legs. I gunned the powerful Volvo down the freeway on-ramp and merged into the flow of predawn traffic, heavy with big rig trucks. I unscrewed the top of the bottle and took a long swig, then I turned up the radio full blast, opened the sunroof, and punched it. The cold and piercing winter air felt marvelous on my flushed face as I pushed through 90, laughing out loud and feeling alive.

I exited the freeway and turned onto a narrow country road. It was dark and wooded. Ahead, the road curved. I took the turn too fast, and reached down with one hand to steady the beer between my legs as the vehicle skidded to the side with a loud screech while the tires strained to grip the pavement. As I pulled out of the turn and back onto the straightaway, a police car coming the other way hit its lights and sirens. I was nailed.

I pulled over hastily, struggling to screw the top back on the beer bottle, and quickly found myself staring up into the flashlight of Officer Gregory of the Boone County Sheriff's Department, who instructed me to pull up my pants and get out of the car. Officer Greg ordered me to dump my beer on the ground, then he performed a field sobriety test which of course I bombed. He put me in the back of his cruiser and proceeded to drive me around for the next two hours asking me questions about my job at Delta and all the places I flew to and the people I met. I thought this was odd but I was very lonely and he was very cute and I was enjoying his company immensely. In hindsight, I realized he was trying to sober me up before taking me in.

Back at the station, Officer Greg fingerprinted and booked me as I sat grinning broadly and waving to everyone who passed by, believing this to be a social call until he told me it was time to descend to the holding cell in the basement, at which point I broke out hysterically sobbing. I was due to pick David up with his car at the airport upon his return off a red-eye flight from San Diego in just a few hours. I knew I was going to be in big trouble. Officer Gregory was unmoved.

David, furious, was waiting for me when I returned home on foot later that evening. I had been charged with DUI and had a pending court date. David and I had a huge fight that got physical and he left to spend the night at a friend's house.

I was certain that everyone, including the Boone County Sheriff's Department, was greatly overreacting. Clearly, this was a giant misunderstanding. But I was scared, very scared. I knew this was bad. Just how bad would not make itself clear for several more years.

I was so excited the night David and I got a trip to Frankfurt together on the magnificent MD-11. I was assigned the First Class galley, my favorite position, working with a very senior, former Pan Am purser, a Dutch woman whose company I enjoyed very much. Much to my delight, First Class was booked empty that night. David was working Business Class with a full load and we counted several friends among the crew.

As we passed over Maritime Canada, we entered an area of strong jet stream winds and the skies became rough. The captain instructed the flight attendants to be seated. Within minutes, the aircraft began a series of rolling undulations which felt like a roller coaster ride, causing passengers to scream as we porpoised across the sky, our stomachs in our throats. I panicked and began to cry as I gripped the galley countertop, frozen and unable to move toward my jumpseat. The kindly purser, who knew a little bit of my story, called David on the intercom and he made his way forward, took me by the hand, and sat me down in the center seats in the middle of the empty First Class cabin where we strapped in to ride out the rough air. I was terrified, and my body was reliving my experience over Lake Michigan from a couple of months earlier. David was reassuring and steady, and seemed to be enjoying the whole affair with a healthy attitude of adventure. He put his arms around me and held me tight while I sobbed and wailed. I was now somewhere between a flashback and a panic attack and quickly losing all control. The purser closed the First Class curtains to give us some privacy and explained to the other crew members what was happening.

When the turbulence subsided shortly thereafter, everyone was so gracious and encouraging to me. But I stayed in my seat for a good half hour, unable to move, nearly catatonic after David went back to work. It was obvious that I was in no condition to continue flying, but without knowledge of PTSD or an appreciation of the severity of the trauma that had been inflicted upon me, I kept soldiering on, retraumatizing myself further and damaging my psyche every time I went up.

The more I experienced fear, flashbacks, and trauma, the more embarrassed and ashamed I felt. Each new event caused me to withdraw further, feeling more isolated and separate from my partner and my friends, the majority of whom were flight attendants enjoying their glamorous lifestyles across the globe, footloose and fancy-free. I internalized everything contrasting my sorrow and despair to their joy and lightness as they came and went without a care. Certainly, I was very broken, consumed by constant and repetitive, obsessive thoughts about flights 800 and 1088, and wrapped up in a constant state of anticipation and cold dread against the next flight ahead. The only thing that provided me a moment's relief from the constant din in my head was the alcohol and so I was drinking around the clock, despite my attendance at mandatory DUI classes and David's hardline stance on drinking in the apartment. I was trying to tow the line at home, to be dutiful and respectful then letting loose in an almost explosive manner on my European layovers. I had gotten so inebriated in Zurich that I had to hide under a parked car to evade some men I had angered in a bar with my belligerent, drunken mouth. Things were clearly spinning beyond control.

Meanwhile, David had his sights set on professional advancement and was awarded a position in Delta's training center in Atlanta. We took a tiny apartment off of Piedmont Park in Midtown, and David went to work at Delta's sprawling headquarters complex, while I gave up my plum international flying and went back to working 727s to Monroe, which left me bitter and resentful. After a few months of discontent, I transferred back to New York, where I could fly international again and began commuting weekly.

One night, on the way back from the airport, a cab driver asked me point-blank if I wanted to buy some coke. I hadn't done cocaine since those late nights in the bars when I first arrived in NYC in my single days. Suddenly, I had something to pick me up when the alcohol stopped working. I was off and running and soon, that taxi cab was pulling up in front of my crash pad apartment at all hours of the night.

My quantum leap into addiction and drug-fueled darkness took place on a Las Vegas layover in 1998. I was purser on the grueling red-eye flight out of JFK that didn't depart until 10 p.m. I had been alone in the crash pad drinking all day, believing that I could stop at a reasonable hour before check-in. I was pleasantly buzzed all the way across the country, and wasted no time in changing and heading out to the Strip upon arrival.

I stumbled into a dive bar where I met a brawny, muscle-bound black man with wide eyes and a twitch. I recognized at once the effects of cocaine, and he became instantly that much more attractive. He chatted me up and quickly asked if I wanted to go home with him. We walked out to the parking lot and got into a big, black Mercedes sedan.

Pulling onto the Strip, he looked over at me and said, "There's some blow in the glove box if you want to do a line." Score. Hungrily, I tore open the glove box, found the little baggy, and laid out a huge rail. Then I pulled a bill out of my wallet, rolled it up, and hit it. My new best friend laughed and nodded his head appreciatively. My nose burned and my eyes watered and I felt my throat close up for a second. This was nothing like I've ever had before. Alarmed, I looked over at the man behind the wheel. "Oh man. That must have been the crystal," he said, and gave me a sly smile. "Hold on, we're almost home," he said, and reached over and squeezed my thigh with a wide grin.

Within seconds, I felt an explosion rock my body. It was as if every nerve in my body caught fire. Consumed by the most exquisite inferno, I was immolated by desire as I reached over and started rubbing the man's strong, broad chest as he drove. There was no controlling myself now, I was completely under the spell of whatever it was I had just ingested. My new friend found all this humorous and laughed out loud. Then he punched the accelerator and sped down Las Vegas Boulevard towards our unknown destination laughing heartily.

I had my hand on the door handle, ready to spring from the car and rip the clothes from my body as we pulled through the ornate stone gates and up a long flagstone driveway of a breathtaking mansion in the desert outside of the city.

I had to blink and clear my eyes for a second look, however, at the sight before me. Although certainly a spectacular home, it had been the recent scene of tactical action. The garage door had been ripped from its flanges and thrown across the driveway. The windows had been smashed out leaving splintered glass strewn about the base of the house. My eyes were instantly drawn to the front door which lay flat in the foyer.

An attractive, young skater boy crept up to the doorway and peered out at us curiously, then darted back into the shadows. "Don't mind the place, we had a little raid," my host explained, as he opened my door and led me up the debris-strewn walkway.

Inside were the remnants of what had once been a fashionable home. Sofas were overturned, tables were smashed, and bookcases upended. The floors were thick with debris and we had to step carefully. The skater boy was now perched on an overturned loveseat, smoking crystal meth from a glass pipe, intent on connecting his torch with the bowl at the end of the pipe. My host rolled his eyes and guided me by the arm through another door-less frame and into a bedroom where a dresser had been thrown on its side and a mirror shattered in pieces on the floor. The bed was devoid of linens and the draperies had been ripped from the window frame.

The man commanded me to get undressed and I pulled my pants and shirt off quickly and obediently. "All the way," he said, and I ripped my underwear off and flung them to the soiled carpet.

He told me to lay on the bed, that he had something in store for me that I was going to love. I laid flat on my back and he reached over my head and pulled a chain from the base of the headboard. In an instant, I was chained and padlocked to the headboard and he was standing over me, feeding me another line of meth off of hand mirror. This was his scene, he said. He liked getting me high. He had to stay sober and dressed he said, to handle his clientele, who by now, were dropping in to make their purchases. He would excuse himself and handle his business in the front of the house, then return with a customer in tow. I was the gift with purchase. Each time I performed admirably, I was locked back up and well rewarded with another line of meth.

In between customers, the skater boy would come and hang in the doorway and look at me, stroking himself and telling me about the girlfriend he wanted to break up with. He said he was 24 and hadn't lived yet. He was constantly in the doorway between rounds, staring and stroking. I never wanted anyone more than I wanted that skater. Our host stood at a distance watching our dance, smiling knowingly and enjoying my torture.

My eyes looked like saucers as I boarded the aircraft shaking and twitching, for the return flight to JFK. There was no way I fooled my crew. I was so sketched out that when the 757 encountered light turbulence over the Rockies, I locked myself in the forward lavatory and stayed there for two hours, leaving my crew to do all the work unsupervised and unassisted. I did not return to Atlanta after that trip, but stayed in New York for a few days trying to regain my composure. I had been introduced to a drug I would chase for the next two decades. It would cause me to lose my mind.

CHAPTER 7

I had barely entered the Upper East Side bar when a platinum-haired, middle-aged man wearing a black leather jacket caught my eye. There was an air of intensity about him, but he gave me a sweet smile. He sat alone nursing a ginger ale and I made my way over and introduced myself. Michael shared that he was a recovering alcoholic, and I tried to pace my vodka tonics, feeling awkward and embarrassed, and mystified that someone could enjoy themselves in a bar without seeking obliteration. At the end of the night, we made plans to meet for dinner at his place when I returned from my next trip a few days later.

Michael's small studio on East 93rd Street was beautifully appointed with antique furnishings, and he prepared an elaborate gourmet meal.

Over dinner, I learned that he was a long-term survivor of AIDS, and had been one of the founders of Act Up. I found his stories of grassroots activism in the early '80s both epic and inspiring. By the end of the evening, I was awash in hero worship. Exhausted from my transatlantic crossing earlier in the day, I started to fade around dessert. Michael drew me a bubble bath and made a cozy bed for me on the sofa, and tucked me in sweetly for the night. He was thoughtful and doting and a perfect gentleman.

The next morning, he walked me to the subway and gave me a kiss on the forehead and put my on the train. Seeing him standing alone in a sea of faces on the platform from the train as it pulled out, I realized I had a new problem.

When David saw the phone bill, which included calls to Michael's New York City phone number, he went ballistic. He was understandably hurt and I didn't have any reasonable explanation to offer. In hindsight I asked myself why I didn't use a calling card. Perhaps on some level, I wanted to get caught. I hadn't been happy in Atlanta, and did not know how to speak up for myself. I put my tail between my legs and bid a hasty retreat back up to New York.

Leaving Atlanta afforded me an opportunity to stand on my own for the first time in my life. I realized that I had gone straight from my parents' home to my marriage, then to cohabitating with a series of lovers. I had yet to live independently. And so I set my sights on an apartment of my own in the city.

It had always been a dream to live in Manhattan and I immersed myself in my search for the perfect place. I found it in Spanish Harlem, in a two-bedroom, 4th floor walk-up on 103rd Street, right off 5th Avenue and Museum Mile, across from the breathtaking Conservatory Gardens of Central Park. It was near the 6 train and the M60 bus which would take me to LaGuardia Airport. It was twice as much each month as our apartment in Atlanta, and I would be doing it by myself each month, but I knew I could just swing it if I flew high time and lived humbly.

I loved everything about living in the city. The twenty-four-hour energy kept me stimulated and engaged. I made interesting and intriguing new friends and there was always something new to try my hand at. I quickly attained my purser qualifications and started flying International again, revisiting familiar, favorite destinations and expanding my horizons each week. My self-esteem soared out from under the weight of a relationship that had grown stagnant and heavy. I was back in my element and truly loving life once more.

But I was not out of danger. It is a testament to my fortitude, resilience, and willpower that I managed to see the world, hold on to my apartment, and maintain a relationship with even mild success while still waging my ongoing, daily battle with PTSD while in the clutches of untreated bipolar and rampant substance abuse. In New York, it was much easier to score drugs like crack and crystal meth than it had been in Kentucky or Atlanta.

Michael became a stabilizing, if not enabling presence and I asked him to move in with me at a grasp at self-preservation. Many late nights I called him collect from some bar or sex club downtown when I lost my wallet or got mugged and had no way home. He always came through, scraping me off the sidewalk at 3 a.m. and shepherding me home in a cab where he drew me a bath and fed me the dinner he prepared while awaiting my call. He ironed my shirts and laid out my uniforms and made sure I got to the airport in the morning. This was a lot to ask of someone in recovery themselves.

Michael was tired. He had been contending with his diagnosis for three decades. He was slowing down. He had beaten cancer but it had taken a toll on his body. He wanted peace and serenity at this stage of his life. He had come far too far to be treated like this.

During the month of August, 2001, I flew the purser position on the JFK to Rome flight, operated with the Boeing 767. On our last trip of the month, my crew briefing was interrupted by the base manager, our stone-faced pilots, and two grave men from Washington, D.C., who informed us that our flight had incurred a "credible threat" by someone named Osama Bin Laden and some group called Al-Qaeda. I scratched my head trying to recall the vaguely familiar name and figured it must have some connection to the World Trade Center bombing in 1993. They explained very detailed safety procedures we would undertake en route and upon arrival in Rome. I found it all very 007 and thought it the height of adventure. We took off for Italy and the flight went off without a hitch.

In the pre-dawn hours of September 10th, 2001, after enjoying a long layover with my dad and stepmom, I strapped myself into the forward jumpseat of an MD-88 and took off from San Antonio headed for Dallas/Fort Worth. We had enjoyed a leisurely evening on the Riverwalk and I looked forward to more trips to Texas in the coming month. Midway between San Antonio and Dallas, we entered an area of severe thunderstorms and the airplane rocked and swayed, gyrating through an explosive, electric sky as lightning flashed all around the aircraft. What made the ordeal worse was knowing that once we landed at DFW, we were to fly the exact same corridor back to San Antonio before continuing on to Atlanta, Washington, D.C., and ultimately JFK. The return flight in a 727 found me cowering on the forward jumpseat, crossing myself and praying that we'd land intact, if at all. While lumbering across the darkened sky in that 727, I decided to file for a leave of absence when we arrived back in New York.

On the morning of September 11th, I awoke late for a 9 a.m. appointment with my therapist on East 11th Street near Washington Square. It was my plan to have him sign off on the leave of absence paperwork which I would then submit to Delta in person at JFK that afternoon. But first, I would take the train down to the World Trade Center do some shopping at Century 21, directly across the street from the twin towers.

I threw on a pair of jeans and a sweatshirt over a t-shirt with the words "Delta Air Lines" in vintage 1940s-style script, and hustled out the door and into the hallway. I had just turned the key in the lock when the phone rang inside and I debated whether I should go back in and answer it. I knew Michael was still asleep so I went back. It was Michael's cousin, Nick, who started the conversation by asking me if I was flying that day. When I replied that I was off for a couple days, he told me a plane had hit the Trade Center and I immediately flipped on the television, phone in hand, and began listening to the reports.

I said goodbye to Nick and woke Michael and we watched in confusion together until that horrific moment when the camera panned to the incoming aircraft and my blood ran cold and my breathing ceased as the inevitable impact became the unfathomable, ghastly visual seared into the world's collective conscience, flashed across every screen across the planet in all its staggering horror until there was nowhere to turn to be free of its savagery. Within minutes, the reporter stated that there were other aircraft missing and expected to impact New York City momentarily. A wave of terror washed over me and I felt desperate and paralyzed as I stood transfixed in my living room only a few hundred yards from 5th Avenue, the magnitude of the present danger consuming me.

Neighbors were now opening their doors and peering into the hallway, and I did the same. We expressed our incredulity at what was occurring just a few miles away. Mount Sinai Hospital was only three blocks away so I and a couple of neighbors walked over to see if we could be of any help and gave blood. Turning the corner onto 5th Avenue, we were greeted with the sobering visage of rows upon rows of empty stretchers lined up side by side down 5th Avenue, awaiting patients. A steady stream of sirens blared down Fifth Avenue.

I needed to walk a bit, to clear my head. I pulled my sweatshirt over my head and tied it around my waist, and set out around the block. As I passed down a tree-lined street in the East 90s, I saw ahead an elderly, hunched woman sitting on her stoop staring ahead sadly. As I approached, we smiled at one another wanly. Her eyes then fell to my t-shirt and the Delta Air Lines logo on my chest. "Young man," she called out softly. I stopped. She struggled to rise tenuously, and I stepped up onto the stoop, and reached out my hand and helped her to her feet slowly. "Terrible," she said and shook her head, distractedly. Her accent was decidedly Eastern European and I wondered what other atrocities this dear woman had witnessed in her time. Then she reached up, this wizened woman who was shorter than me, and took my face into her hands. Her hands were weathered but warm. She looked me in the eye. Her eyes were blue and bright and clear. "Perhaps if there was a strong young boy like you on that airplane, they could have been stopped." Then she sighed, "Meh, who's to say," and gave a shrug.

Later in the day, I wandered down to the bodega on the corner and huddled around the transistor radio with the two Yemeni brothers who owned the place. We cried together and the younger brother asked me if I thought people would hate them now.

Once the towers fell, it became too much to bear and I had to get out of the apartment and away from the television. I grabbed a bottle of wine from my refrigerator and wandered across Fifth Avenue and into Central Park where I met up with, until then, unknown neighbors for what became an impromptu celebration of life. We toasted those lost, we toasted our city, and we toasted life. New Yorkers, when speaking of 9/11, will make mention of the crystal blue sky and cool breeze that made it one of the most spectacular days in recollection. We noted the day's beauty as we sat cross-legged on the grass sipping wine and feeling guilty for savoring perhaps the most beautiful day any could recall even as such horror and devastation was unfolding just a few miles down the Avenue. From our idyllic spot on the vast lawn, we saw the putrid smoke billowing above the tree line and smelled the acrid stench of burning plastic that filled the sky. Soon, we heard the eerie whine of high altitude jet engines as fighter jets began to circle Manhattan, too high to be spotted by the naked eye.

When the airports reopened, my first trip back was on September 17th, a 767 to Madrid. I could not have handpicked a better crew, comprised of old friends and fellow New York City residents. We carried only 44 passengers that night and had to return to the departure gate twice to discharge frightened passengers. I worked the forward galley, where the first atrocities had occurred on the hijacked airliners

a week earlier and my heart broke for the hero flight attendants and first responders who fought darkness so valiantly in their final moments.

My next trip was to Paris with a particularly raucous and rowdy group of flyers I truly adored. We went to dinner at Ferdinand's, my favorite Parisian bistro, where we consumed copious amounts of red wine. We were obnoxious no doubt, blowing off steam and letting loose after the stress and anxiety of recent events. I noticed the French diners in the restaurant grow uncomfortable and glance at our table from time to time. Finally, a refined, attractive Frenchman stood up from his table and began to cross the dining room, heading towards us. Anticipating a scolding, I tensed.

"You are American, no?" the man asked the table. Chastened, I replied that yes, we were American, and that we were a flight crew from

New York. I explained that we had a rough time recently, and apologized for disrupting his evening.

"No, my friends, I have come only to extend our sympathies. And to say that the hearts of France weep with those of America tonight."

Immediately following 9/11, Delta slashed 1,400 flight attendant positions from the New York City base. Suddenly, I was back to domestic flying, covering all three New York area airports with a drastic reduction in salary. In addition to my escalating PTSD, I was now contending with new and stressful responsibilities on the airplane. Flight attendants had become the first line of defense in a new war on terror. Each flight brought unprecedented challenges and fears.

At the urging of my therapist, I decided to take a break from flying at last. I put in for a six-month leave of absence and my father agreed to help supplement my income. I decided to go back to school and was ecstatic when a placement test at NYU's School of Professional and Continuing Studies recommended I take the fourth-year, advanced Spanish course despite my not having studied the language in over a decade. I loved being on campus, and I felt stimulated and engaged amongst the bright and ambitious, youthful student body. The class was fast-paced and challenging under the instruction of our sharp-witted, Argentinian professor and was unlike any classroom experience I had before. I started attending 12-step meetings again and seeing my therapist weekly, and soon I was able to put together a period of abstinence which allowed me to really begin to unravel some of the trauma and PTSD. I even joined the famous YMCA immortalized in the song by the Village People. Regular workouts, combined with the Atkins diet, which was all the rage, allowed me to get into top physical shape for the first time in years. Michael was happy with my progress as well, and our home life settled into a happy routine. It seemed I was finally finding some peace at last.

I grew optimistic about my return to flying. When schedules came out for the month ahead, I was delighted to see that I had been awarded the Paris trip which was a very simple 3-on, 4-off schedule with a 24-hour layover in Paris each week. I could not have asked for a better return. I finished my course at NYU with an A+ and prepared to return to work.

A few days before my first trip back, however, I started feeling anxious. I had trouble sleeping, which I chalked up to excitement.

I flew my first trip over and it went well. It felt great to be back on the airplane, and I flew with several of my friends. But that also meant dining at Etoile Verte, a favorite crew hangout where we were always met with a round of Kir Royale when we walked into the place. So much for sobriety. There had been no resolve. A few bottles of red wine circulated around the table, and as always, a few of us had gone out for a nightcap afterwards. It had all been very civilized. The flight home had been flawless, which had only served to embolden me. I pushed the envelope on the next trip, again making the rounds with my crew, then slipping back out after everyone had gone to bed.

Twas the night before Halloween and my friend Kevin was on the phone. Kevin lived in Midtown and was my connect and fuckbuddy. A couple times a month, he would come up and spend a weekend with me locked away in a drug-fueled bacchanalian. Mild-mannered, middle-aged accountant by day, Kevin had his finger on the pulse of the city's underground sex and drug scene by night and knew all the players and the purveyors who enabled our weekend staycations. He had just scored some good crystal meth and wanted to come over. I knew I shouldn't give in, as I was scheduled to fly back to Paris the next night. But Michael was away for the week and crystal could be hard to find in the city. I took it when I could get it.

Besides, if it got out of hand, I could always call in sick, even though I was out of sick time for the year already. But calling out on Halloween would require a doctor's note, and there was no way I could come up with that on such short notice. I debated for a minute, then I gave in as usual. In short order, Kevin was pushing past me into the doorway and laying out his favors, pipes, and sex toys on my bed. Meth, GHB, ketamine, he had it all. This was going to be a hell of a show. With Kevin, it always was. So much in fact that I spiraled into deep depression whenever he left.

I spent the next 24 hours flying high, trying to ignore the fact that my employer expected me to do just that shortly. When I could delay no longer, I pushed Kevin and his bag of tricks out the door, cleaned myself up, and shoved off for JFK.

Landing in Paris the next morning, I headed straight out to do some day drinking at Le Depot, a seamy bar-come-sex club in the Marais where I stayed until sundown. I headed back to the hotel and met up with some of my crew downstairs in the bar for drinks and dinner followed by a nightcap at an Irish pub across from the hotel. Had I called it a night at that point, I might have been okay, at least for another day. I may have slipped under the radar yet one more time. But it was Halloween night and I couldn't see sitting alone watching CNN when the party of the year was ramping up just outside my door. Instead, I decided to see what was brewing at the Banque Club, a bar built on top of an S&M dungeon off the Champs Elysees. I snuck back downstairs, hailed a cab, and sped off into the Parisian night.

Once inside the darkened bar, I ordered a drink. I was drinking for effect now so I slammed it down and ordered another. The lean, muscled bartender in his tight, white t-shirt raised an eyebrow as he set down the second vodka tonic before me. I threw that one back as well, and motioned for a third. He crossed his arms and leaned against the bar behind me and said something in scornful French, smiling patronizingly. The room was spinning and I was now sufficiently primed to explore the various moans and sighs coming from the dungeon below. I climbed down off my seat, righted myself, and wobbled off towards the stairs that descended into the dimly lit chambers below.

I had no idea what time it was as the faint glow of the rising sun crept beneath the front door. I was naked sitting atop the bar, my legs intertwined with those of a sinewy, young Frenchman as we fumbled clumsily in a drunken spectacle as I came back to consciousness. Just below and to the side of us, a second Parisian sat on a bar stool, sans pants, cheering us on in slurred French. The hot and scornful bartender once again leaned against the bar with his arms folded, eyebrow raised, a bemused expression across his face. The bar was otherwise empty. The ménage a trois continued while the barman scrubbed and polished and swept around us unfazed by the whole affair. At length, he called it a night, and locked the front door. The three of us, who had been otherwise occupied, pulled on our clothes and followed the sexy bartender out the side door and into the alley where a motorcycle sat parked against a wall.

My playmates bid us adieu and I hung back in the pale light and cool shade of the alley breathing in the clean morning air, hoping to savor the moment a second longer. The bartender stood in front of me now, achingly beautiful and ever masculine in his black leather jacket, jeans, and boots. He ran his hand through his wavy, sandy blond hair, and smiled sheepishly. Suddenly, he looked nervous and shy, no longer imposing and hard as he had in the bar. He looked down and shifted from one foot to the other. Then he reached inside his jacket and pulled out a joint, raised it to me, and smiled. My pulse quickened. This meant he wanted the moment to linger, too. I knew I couldn't smoke with him. Even though I was blasted on crystal meth and had about a gallon of vodka in my bloodstream, I was due on the airplane in less than three hours. I shrugged my shoulders and shook my head and he lit the joint and took a hit. He leaned his head back and exhaled. His shoulders dropped. He began trying to speak to me in very bad English, stammering and searching for words. He was adorable. We established that I lived in New York and I somehow made clear that I found him extremely sexy. We stood there grinning sheepishly at one another feeling stupid for another minute. I said a lot of inane things in a combination of English and weak French, none of which he understood, yet he smiled and nodded eagerly as if every word was fucking brilliant. He was a study in masculine perfection as he mounted his bike, a French James Dean crossed with a Da Vinci angel.

He gave me a sweet smile and a nod then kicked the starter and revved the bike. Then he waved, raced up the alley and onto the street, leaving me flushed and short of breath.

I was feeling no pain when I slipped that first red wine split into my apron high above the North Atlantic a few hours later. I was standing alone in the galley having run back to retrieve some supplies for the bar cart in the aisle when I realized that I could easily slip into the lavatory and down a quick drink and be back up the aisle before anyone would know the difference. It was risky and dangerous for sure, and that was half the attraction. Once I had gotten away with it, I was hooked on the thrill. A few rows later, I created another catering emergency that required me to run to the galley once more. Soon, the service was over and half the crew was on a rest break meaning I only had one or two crew members to maneuver around in the back of the airplane. Getting in and out of the lavatory would be much simpler now. I was on a mission for maximum inebriation. Midway through the flight, I did shots with a couple of French college kids in the back galley and I enjoyed some red wine and a long-winded conversation with a good-natured passenger in business class which was odd considering I was working coach. I enjoyed this flight far more than any in recent memory.

Suddenly, we were on the ground at JFK and my friends, who I flew this trip with every week, were gathered around me in the back of the now-empty airplane as I argued belligerently that I was perfectly capable of walking unassisted down the jetway and into the customs hall.

I stormed ahead, seeing double, and waddled off the aircraft and into the stream of humanity headed for customs and baggage claim. Once in the massive arrivals hall, I took my place in the crew line and leaned heavily against my luggage in an attempt at remaining upright. When motioned forward, I tripped and stumbled hard against the counter.

"Whoa, Buddy," the inspector exclaimed as he shot backwards blinded by my hundred-proof breath. He motioned to two burly Port Authority cops who quickly came over and sized up the situation. The inspector asked me for my passport which, in my drunken stupor, I had neglected to remove from my bag.

"Sure thing!" I slurred amiably (I was a happy drunk that day). I crouched down to open my bag and promptly fell over sideways onto the floor. I laid there for a beat as the room span around me and it dawned on me that this was a very dire turn of events. I scrambled, limbs akimbo, to grab hold of my wheeled suitcase and right myself, aware of the mounting attention from passengers and my fellow crew behind me. I felt sick. I squinted, trying to find the zipper to open my tote bag but my double vision was so bad I couldn't find the tab. I turned the tote upside but could not figure out how to open it as my anxiety ratcheted up into sheer panic.

"What are you, fuckin' DRUNK?" roared a beefy, red-faced, Irish cop now towering directly over me as another cop reached down and grabbed me from under the arms, yanking me to my feet.

"YER FUCKIN CRAZY!" the cop spat in my face as I began to shake like a leaf. "YA' FUCKIN STUPID FUCK! WOULD YA LOOK AT THIS STUPID FUCK!" the cop barked out across the crowded customs hall as 3,000 passengers suddenly turned, fell silent, and stared open-mouthed at the spectacle unfolding. Suddenly, I was loudly ordered to step away from my luggage and told not to move. Someone from Delta was on the way to collect me, I was told.

"YOU'RE FUCKED NOW, BUDDY!" I heard someone yell from afar as even more cops descended upon me. I began to cry.

CHAPTER 8

I was quickly escorted to Delta's offices across the terminal where we were joined by the base manager for an impromptu conference. Unlike most major airlines, Delta's flight attendants did not enjoy the benefits of union representation. Therefore, there was no one to accompany me for the conversation, no one to guarantee I was treated fairly or to ensure I did not incriminate myself in any way. I felt overwhelmed and frightened, embarrassed and ashamed. But Delta had always asserted an "open door" policy and took the company at face value. I vowed to be as transparent and cooperative as possible. This would prove to be a big mistake.

Both the base manager and the supervisor seemed genuine and sympathetic and authentically concerned. Immediately, the base manager pointed out that my hand was bleeding. She asked how I had injured myself, but I had no recollection of doing so. It was obvious that I was intoxicated and I did not deny it. When asked if I had been drinking, I acknowledged it readily.

I explained that I was experiencing a lot of anxiety flying after 9/11. I talked about living in Manhattan and about my experience of that day. For the first time, I opened up and talked about the severe turbulence encounter out of Chicago and how badly that had affected me. I shared that I was seeing a therapist each week, working through that issue. I said that I was disappointed by the company's lack of support. I talked about how difficult flying and caretaking for Michael was proving to be.

I admitted that all of this was too much for me and that it had led me to make this bad decision. I held nothing back.

The managers asked if I wanted help and I readily agreed. They told me a representative from EAP would be in touch in the morning and that he could arrange treatment. In that moment, I felt such relief. I was exhausted from months of the juggling act that had become my life and I so wanted a way out. I was truly grateful for the offer of help.

Of course I asked about my job. I was told that while no promises could be made, once I completed treatment, there would be a review. I was assured that flight attendants who complied with all facets of rehabilitation were quite often reinstated. I expressed my gratitude and my commitment and we adjourned. I headed back to the city and waited to hear from EAP in the morning.

At the appointed hour the next morning, I climbed into a town car and headed out to the Hamptons to begin a 28-day rehab stay. I grabbed my overnight bag and walked into the lobby where I was greeted warily by three curious patients.

"What's your D.O.C?" asked an intense and nervous, thirty-something emergency room nurse in combat boots with a pageboy haircut

"Huh?" I replied, confused.

"It means 'Drug of Choice,'" laughed Elenora, a middle-aged woman with an elegant English accent who turned out to be a British Airways flight attendant who would become my partner-in-crime.

"Oh, well I drink too much. And I do some crystal. I mean, sometimes I do a little," I said.

At this point in my life I was nowhere ready to look inward and acknowledge the ravages that crystal meth was having on my life. I truly believed it was something I was able to do a weekend a month with Kevin then go on with my regularly scheduled life. I couldn't admit that crystal meth, combined with my yet-undiagnosed bipolar disorder, was taking me to the depths of depression and had me borderline suicidal. For quite some time, I tried to quit drinking and had hatched elaborate schemes to get through the day without picking up a drink. But meth still seemed a big sexy adventure to me. Crystal meth was still new in New York City and I would be the first crystal meth patient to attend this rehab. They weren't sure what to do with me when I arrived on the scene.

Standing solemnly in this trio was a beautiful, muscle-bound, thirty-something with downcast eyes and a sweet, sad smile. Craig was a Port Authority police sergeant who escaped the collapse of the North Tower and had been one of the few survivors from his station house. He would become a big brother to me and I always found comfort and safety by his side. NYPD and NYFD sent dozens of men to this rehab during my stay. I found them so heroic and noble as they faced their demons and trauma head-on in the wake of unimaginable horrors.

Here I learned the connection between trauma and addiction. It was no coincidence that we had all flamed out just months after 9/11. We were all first responders who all had jobs that subjected us to heightened anxiety every single day. We had all soldiered on saying nothing until the day we could go no further. I also learned about the genetic predisposition to alcoholism and substance abuse. I came from a long line of addicted men so of course I would end up in rehab at some point in time.

I took to treatment like a duck to water. I loved everything about it. Within days, the drugs and alcohol out of my system, I felt a new vitality and a lightness of being. It is said that "tragedy plus time equals comedy" and my new friends and I found great hilarity in the insanity of our life situations. We sat drinking coffee in the cafeteria until the pre-dawn hours howling over the calamitous situations that brought us into treatment.

A new character joined our group a week into my stay. Mark was twenty-six, an electrician from the city and the father of two young girls. He had a brooding intensity and seethed with anger. But he was quick-witted with a keen intellect and I enjoyed his company. Mark had marginal success at recovery in the past but had recently relapsed. Now, he was extremely hard on himself for it and could not find self-forgiveness. I identified with the perfectionist in Mark and we became close, often taking long walks in the evening and getting into deep philosophical talks about recovery and our hopes for the future. More than anything, Mark wanted to turn his life around and be a good father to the two young girls he adored.

Each week, I checked in with my counselor and we called my EAP representative at Delta who relayed a report to management. My counselor felt I was making fabulous progress and I couldn't be any more excited for the future. As my treatment came towards the close, we made a plan for my return to work. We acknowledged the triggers and temptations that I would face back on the line, all the things that had derailed me in Paris after that first leave of absence, and we shared our plan with my EAP rep. Delta still hadn't given me an answer either way but as I had been completely compliant with their directions and had excelled in treatment, no one saw any reason why I wouldn't go right back on the line at the end of the month.

My counselor tried to prepare me for all possible scenarios, reminding me that the possibility remained that I could face unemployment at the end of treatment. Yet, I knew other flight attendants who had been disciplined for substance abuse violations and been reinstated. Every other airline offered a second chance. Certainly this would be the case here as well, I assumed. Yet, I acknowledged this reality, and worked hard to get into acceptance around it. I surrendered to the situation and prayed, "Thy will be done." Word came back through my EAP rep that my supervisor would come to the rehab to meet with me on my last day of treatment.

The night before, I went through my graduation ceremony which was emotional and heartwarming. Mark, myself, and another patient, Jose, received our diplomas and prepared to return to the city in the morning. I went to bed feeling healthy, accomplished, and looking forward to reconnecting with my supervisor, John, who I knew would be proud of my progress as well.

I awoke early and dressed in the early morning, excited for the day and the future ahead. Adding to the excitement, it was my 33rd birthday. My friends thought it strange that my supervisor would drive three hours to the rehab just to tell me that I could come back to work. In my excitement, I missed the meaning in their insistence upon awaiting my supervisor's arrival with me in the lobby.

I met with John, the EAP rep, and my counselor in the office and we got right down to business. John told me I looked great and that he had been pleased with the reports he received. He was happy to see I was doing so well.

Then without missing a beat, he opened his briefcase, pulled out a typed document, and pushed it towards me. It was a formal letter of resignation with my name typed at the bottom. "Delta has decided not to continue your employment. But we would like to give you this opportunity to resign." I had known this was a possibility but that did not stop my heart from shattering to the floor. I looked down at the proffered resignation letter, unable to meet anyone's eyes as tears welled in my own. There were some conciliatory words offered but I didn't hear a thing as I picked up the pen and scribbled my name tersely.

Suddenly, everyone was joyfully retiring to the dining room for lunch and a facility tour as I sat behind with my counselor trying to make sense of the heartbreak and betrayal that had just occurred.

I arrived home to an empty apartment. Michael had moved out in the aftermath of my drunken unmanageability. I sat in the window looking out upon the snow drifts below until darkness fell over the street. The phone rang. It was Mark. We commiserated a bit on our less than stellar homecomings.

He said he owed somebody $200 and asked if I could loan it to him until payday. I agreed and we made plans to meet at the Port Authority bus terminal in an hour. When we met, Mark seemed agitated and anxious, in a hurry to get out of there. I chalked it up to the stress of being back in the city and I headed home.

The next morning, I was awoken by the ringing telephone. It was Jose. Mark was dead. Overdosed on heroin. Jose was confused. Mark was out of work and had no money for drugs. I was sick to my stomach. He left behind his two beautiful girls.

There is a dirty little secret in recovery that nobody tells you. Once you put down the poison, things get worse before they get better. I faced my new future alone, unemployed, and grieving Mark while feeling responsible for his death as well. A quick glance at my finances told me I would quickly lose my apartment if I didn't do something fast.

I walked into the human resource department of Bloomingdale's 59th Street flagship store and filled out an application. When I handed it back to the receptionist, she smiled and said, "Oh, you were a flight attendant? I flew for Eastern. Let me see what I can do here." I credit Muriel for launching me on what turned into a fabulous second career just in the nick of time. Within minutes, I was interviewing with the manager of the men's department who was excited about my former management experience with the Broadway. I started training the next day.

Within a couple of months, I was recruited by Burberry and I became the boutique manager in short order, reporting directly to Burberry London and making more than I did flying internationally with Delta. Bloomingdale's was great fun and there was always something exciting happening on the main floor of the iconic store. I was invited to fashion shows and worked behind the scenes in the Burberry showrooms. I had a celebrity clientele and worked with the United Nations, diplomats, and customers from across the globe. It was glamorous, high fashion work, and I loved every minute of it.

I made an honest attempt at recovery and held it together for several months until I met a captivating and sensual man who turned out to be the harbinger of the struggle that would define my life for years ahead. Brad was a former pro football player-turned-physician. With chiseled good looks and an impressive linebacker's build, he was a fantasy incarnate when I met him in a club late one night. We quickly stole away to his immaculate Brooklyn brownstone where we made love. He asked if I partied and my resolve for sobriety instantly evaporated beneath the spell cast by his breathtaking manhood.

Brad told me to wait a moment and slipped out of bed and into the kitchen. When he returned, he held two syringes in the palm of his hand. He asked me if I'd ever "slammed" before. I didn't really know what he was talking about, but the implication was clear. I knew I was in over my head but I would have done anything to prolong the moment with this spectacular man. Plus, he was a doctor, so what could possibly go wrong?

Brad told me to put out my arm and I went with it. He instructed me to look away as he nimbly and gingerly handled the syringe. Suddenly, there was a flash and a bang and a deafening rush in my ears and I was consumed by the most delicious heat as my body arched upward almost off the mattress. I fought to catch my breath as I was suddenly overtaken by the most powerful and compelling lust I had ever known. I experienced a hundred orgasms in one and every cell in my body screamed out in ecstasy. Within seconds, he had shot himself up as well and suddenly, he was on me and in me and I knew my life would never be the same. I could never settle for anything less than this again.

When I finally emerged from Brad's brownstone two days later, I was exhausted, dehydrated, and spent. I tried to go back to work but I was so weak I couldn't make it through the day and my manager sent me to the hospital where I was admitted overnight. It was the first time I had ever been hospitalized because of my drug use. It would be far from the last.

Freed from the rigors of the mandatory drug testing that came with my flight attendant job, my drug use exploded exponentially. I was now in the grips of a full-blown addiction. I had found my way into the rooms of Crystal Meth Anonymous and I was making a very concerted effort, attending meetings, meeting with a sponsor, and working the 12 steps. But I was no match for a drug that burned brighter than the sun when injected into my body.

I was now single and unencumbered with no accountability for the first time in years. I began making the rounds to the bars, adult theaters, and sex clubs downtown in what would become a near nightly ritual that lasted until sunrise. It seemed I could never be satiated and the drug only fueled the rampage.

Somewhere along the way, a trick turned me on to huffing Dust

Off. When sprayed on a rag and inhaled, it created a rush followed by a euphoria and ultimately led to a blackout. Since my life had become so meaningless and empty, oblivion had a certain allure at this point and I took to huffing a dozen or more cans a night.

The downside to Dust Off was that being a solvent, it was highly caustic. Some of the solution would gather in my stomach, and it would cause painful retching and vomiting. After a few cans, it would burn and freeze my vocal cords and seer my lungs. Yet I became highly addicted both to the euphoric state the substance afforded me and the painful and degrading physical suffering I experienced when using it. My use of inhalants took a masochistic and sordid twist when it crossed a line into self-mutilation and I began to get off on the pain and suffering I was putting my body through. I achieved my highest state of bliss when I reached agony and the whole thing became about getting off by inflicting harm on myself. Nirvana was reached if I could extract bile from my stomach before blacking out. It was an appalling form of self-torture that took months of therapy to unpack and understand. Self-loathing in the extreme.

My new addiction nearly killed me one night when I inhaled 72 cans in a video booth of an adult book store in Times Square. I had passed out and fell to the floor where I remained overnight, my left side paralyzed. I spent three nights at St. Vincent's Hospital before I could walk and it was as a week before I had full use of my left arm or could speak clearly.

On July 12th, 2005, I tested positive for HIV at the Callen Lorde Community Health Clinic in New York City. Kevin was waiting for me in the lobby. Kevin pushed his 10-speed bicycle beside me as I walked up the West Side Highway trying to come to terms with my new reality. It came as no surprise. I knew I would have to make adjustments if I wanted to remain healthy. I would think about that later. We went back to my place, got high, and fucked.

In addition to out-of-control sexual compulsion, I was grappling with ever more turbulent mood swings and more irrational irritability than ever. I knew the drugs and alcohol had a lot to do with this but I couldn't help but wonder if there was more to the story, and I was scared. Finally, at Michael's suggestion, I made an appointment with a psychiatrist who quickly diagnosed me with bipolar disorder. While it made perfect sense and explained so many things, like the hypersexuality, I was deeply embarrassed and ashamed by the diagnosis, even more so than I was by that of the HIV. The doctor prescribed lithium and reiterated the importance of abstinence, or at least cutting back on my drinking if I was to get the upper hand on my mental health.

The trifecta of psych meds, abstinence, and 12-step recovery work served me well and I entered into an era of relative peace that lasted for quite some time. I got back to the gym and adhered to my HIV medication regimen and focused on my career aspirations at the store. I began to travel again and joined some friends for some fabulous trips to San Tropez and Tuscany.

In 2005, my father was diagnosed with ALS, a heartbreaking and tragic degenerative disease, and I began commuting between New York and Texas to visit and assist with his care. With each of us facing our own mortalities, we bonded in a way we never had before. In the eighteen months he lived following his diagnosis, we were able to share and communicate openly and honestly, which was new for our relationship. I was present during his last days and we left nothing unsaid.

CHAPTER 9

Five years had passed since I was unceremoniously dumped by Delta, and I had come a long way. With each passing airplane, I looked skyward and wondered if it might be possible to return to the skies. I began to research what airlines were hiring and started sending out resumes. I landed a few interviews where I was honest and transparent and shared my story with the recruiters, who were compassionate and appreciative. In each instance, they encouraged me and escalated my application to human resources, where it was always shot down.

At length, I was invited to a group interview with JetBlue Airways in November, 2007. I arrived at corporate headquarters determined to give it my best but not expecting much. The interview was the typical cattle call and I offered a few highly forgettable words about myself, then headed out to JFK and flew home to California for the holidays, putting the whole affair to the back of my mind. I arrived back in New York a week later to a letter offering me a position in an upcoming training class in Orlando. I had my second chance at last.

Teaching an old dog new tricks was tough. What had taken seven weeks at Delta was accomplished in three at JetBlue. I struggled to unlearn years of prior training so that I could absorb JetBlue's procedures fresh. At the end of the course, we were pinned our wings and given our diplomas in the auditorium as Tina Turner's "Simply the Best" blared from the loudspeakers and friends and family cheered from the stands, including Ken, my new boyfriend of a few months. The next morning, I boarded my flight back to JFK, my new base.

A nor'easter pounded the city with no signs of letting up as I inched my way up the Belt Parkway towards the airport to report for my training flight to Orlando and back. Once onboard with the working crew and my two fellow trainees, the cockpit crew conducted the pre-flight briefing and informed us we could expect lengthy delays and rough skies all the way to Florida and back. My anxiety began to rise.

Once the passengers were seated and we pushed back from the gate, I performed the safety demo in the aisle like the veteran flight attendant I was. Soon, de-icing trucks began to spray the aircraft with their solution and my anxiety ratched up another notch.

I was seated on the forward jumpseat when we began our takeout roll and lifted off into a blinding white sky. Within a few hundred feet, the aircraft began to shutter and buffet in heavy turbulence as we climbed up through the powerful winter storm. My heart leapt into my throat and I prayed this wouldn't last more than a few minutes of our climb-out. The aircraft still rocked and bucked at 10,000 when the captain called back and said he didn't expect it to improve but if we wanted to serve we could.

I slipped into the forward lavatory and splashed some water on my face. I was terrified. All the panic and anxiety of my flying past came flooding back and I realized I had made a huge mistake. Five years away from the industry had done absolutely nothing to heal my PTSD. I simply could not do this job. Outside the lavatory door in the forward galley were two flight attendants and two trainees waiting for me to join them to begin the service. I had no choice but to go through with this horror show. I prayed for strength, dried my face, and opened the door.

We tried to serve the frightened passengers but the turbulence was so rough that we could serve only a couple rows then had to take our seats. I was on the verge of a full-blown panic attack the entire flight. By the time we touched down in Florida, I was near tears and the worst part was knowing we had to board up and do this once more. I got off the airplane at JFK that afternoon knowing I had a huge problem on my hands with no idea what to do about it.

Everything had changed in the airline industry in the five years that I had been away. JetBlue had built its success on being a "low-cost carrier." They wrote the book on doing more with less. Where Delta was a major international carrier with vast resources and a staff of a hundred thousand spread across the globe, JetBlue expected its flight attendants to clean the airplanes in between flights on short, unrealistic turnarounds. Gone were the days of working one flight to the West Coast, spending 24 sundrenched hours by the pool, and working one luxurious non-stop home. Now, flight crews regularly flew from New York to Los Angeles and right back in a single, grueling shift, often doing so several days in a row. Toward the end of my career with Delta, I was flying a beautiful 3-day on, 4-day off schedule with 48-hour layovers in Brussels or Stockholm. Now I was back on call, covering three New York City airports, and often receiving my flight assignments at 3:30 in the morning. JetBlue was positively abusive in their scheduling of flight attendants. It was not uncommon to be assigned a simple one-day turnaround only to have it extended upon arrival for up to four or five days.

Working for JetBlue was exhausting and demoralizing and I did not do well in this new environment. There simply wasn't time for self-care and my 12-step meetings and regular sessions with my psychiatrist, the foundations of my recovery program, were the first items slashed. I began running at high anxiety, with lack of sleep taking a heavy toll on my body in addition to the multiple time zones I was crossing each week. I was in dangerous territory.

Bipolar disorder is a sly and stealthy, constant companion that may lurk scheming beneath the surface of a seemingly placid psyche for decades, lulling the victim into a false state of security with its seeming surrender. To friends and colleagues, the bipolar appears to be the one who has it all together, gifted even, and his ability to juggle a dizzying array of interests and ambitions with skill and ease earns praise. But much the way a violent earthquake is preceded by a series of fissures deep within the earth's crust, he may start to show subtle cracks if only inward, hairline fractures visible only with the magnifying glass of self-awareness and hard-won insight gleaned from surviving years of seismic upheaval.

He knows about Bipolar. He has been diagnosed by the leading specialists in the field. He has taken countless medications, kept up with blood tests and Lithium levels. He appreciates the gravity of his situation.

He recalls with chagrin that day he found himself at the Bloomingdale's jewelry counter unable to stop himself from blowing his hard-earned rent money on rose-gold David Yurman rings and cable-wire bracelets without a second thought to where he would lay his head in the weeks to come. And that crazy morning in Los Angeles when he ran out for milk and came home with a forest green Mini Cooper instead. He can't forget how he smashed his laptop with a hammer in a fit of rage and threw the shattered remnants from the 4th floor window of his Upper East Side apartment to the street below. And he can still bring back to consciousness the harrowing moment he took leave of his body and observed himself from somewhere behind as he stomped down on the accelerator and aimed his car dead ahead on an intractable collision course with another car. The sharp jolt of electricity in his brain snapped his head from side to side as the deafening screech of tearing metal filled the vehicle and pulled him back to reality. It was shortly after that "accident" that he sought help from a psychiatrist and came to terms with his diagnosis.

It had all made sense then, and he took the news gravely and vowed to apply his new self-awareness in earnest. Thus, he knows better than to surrender to the sweet, sinister seduction of an elusive, subtle, and seemingly innocuous elation which never ends in anything but a frightful, uncontrolled descent into chaos and unmanageability.

Yet, his disease, an ever-lurking predator which lies in wait in the most obscure recesses of his otherwise self-possessed mind, sometimes catches him at a rare moments of complacency and fatigue and whispers seductively, harkening back to more adventurous and exhilarating, carefree days.

Maybe he missed a follow-up appointment or somehow missed a pill or two, and then a refill, maybe two. Perhaps it was the weekly transcontinental commute. Or maybe, he just felt better and for one minute he forgot. Forgot about the jewelry and the Mini Cooper and the eviction and the drinking and the hammer and the crash...and just allowed himself to be like everyone else.

But he wasn't like everyone else. And something had shifted. When, he couldn't quite say, but it had, although almost imperceptibly at first.

Yet for all its stress and strain, I loved being back in the skies, in my element. I treasured the real human connections I was making with my passengers each week. I loved the unaccompanied minors, the newlyweds, the seniors. I understood that not everyone traveled for joy and I extended myself to comfort the grieving. I got involved in service committees and was elected Chairman of the Uniform Redesign Committee, overseeing the creation of a new uniform for all frontline employees. I worked on committees dealing with quality of work-life issues, scheduling concerns, and safety improvements. I worked at headquarters on numerous special assignments as well. I loved learning about the industry from behind the scenes and from the corporate side of things.

The phone rang in the pre-dawn hours and I was offered the opportunity to fly a mission to New Orleans in advance of hurricane Gustave, which was barreling down on the city at rapid speed. The idea was to ferry an empty A320 ahead of the storm and evacuate 150 stranded passengers who had been in the airport for 24 hours, abandoned by TSA. We would also carry food and relief supplies to be unloaded upon arrival. Ours would be the last aircraft to arrive in New Orleans and most poignantly, the last to depart before the storm made landfall. Of course I jumped at the opportunity and headed to the airport immediately.

At the departure gate, we met up with a cavalcade of volunteers including JetBlue executives, ramp and customer service agents, and headquarters personnel who would join us for the flight. The plan was for our volunteer ground staff to relieve the local New Orleans staff so they could return home before the storm fell. The New York-based ground crew would work the departure of the flight, then jump on at the last minute.

We took off into the inky darkness and headed towards New Orleans at top speed, not knowing quite what to anticipate further south. Tensions were high but so were our spirits and there was much laughter in the cabin as we all got acquainted. Approaching New Orleans, the cabin grew quiet as the sky grew darker, each of us remembering the devastation wrought by Katrina not long ago.

By the time we landed, power had been lost in the terminal, and we deplaned using a set of mobile stairs. Our volunteer ground staff deplaned first and quickly went to work processing the passengers by hand while the others began unloading the relief supplies, then began the task of loading the passengers' luggage into the cargo hold.

All the restaurants and shops in the airport had been long closed leaving the drinking fountains and taps in the restrooms the only amenities available to the stranded passengers. I and the other two flight attendants quickly went to work in the forward galley loading trays with juice, bagels, and cups of sliced fruit which we then circulated through the terminal amongst the stranded passengers. We were able to feed every soul in the terminal with the supplies we carried in from New York.

Climbing out into the dark and brooding sky, we looked down upon the helpless and vulnerable city below. Stretching as far as the eye could see sat stalled, red tail lights in the direct path of the virulent storm. There were many tears amongst the 150 grateful refugees as we all absorbed the enormity and gravity of the moment. We did our best to make our passengers feel like honored guests despite the heartbreaking circumstances of their travel. The journey was at turns both joyful and tragic but it was above all, a profoundly human experience. I am so appreciative to have been a part of this life-changing mission. And for that, I will always be grateful to JetBlue.

Ken and I decided to move in together and we set our sights on a beach house in Belle Harbor in the Rockaways near JFK. The house we found was perfect. Two bedrooms, with a beautiful stretch of white sandy beach at our doorstep. We moved in in the summer of 2008. Belle Harbor was a beautiful community of gracious homes, tree-lined streets, and a picturesque harbor. It was a touch of the Hamptons a stone's throw from the city and JFK. I bought myself a brand new Jeep and we had a crew of great friends among the local recovery community. It was moonlight swims and beach bonfires every weekend. Life was truly idyllic.

Ken and I were about to depart on a seven-day Caribbean cruise when my mother called from California. She had been admitted to the hospital in terrible pain, her joints inflamed, nearly immobile. We called off the cruise and I jumped on the first flight out to Los Angeles. As a precaution, my mom was seen by an oncologist who ran a series of tests, including a biopsy, of a mass on her lungs. My mother had quit smoking fifteen years earlier and other than diabetes (which she had under control), was a relatively well woman so we weren't too terribly alarmed by the whole affair.

While casually flipping through the channels on the overhead television in her room one afternoon, a news report came on about an A320 aircraft down in New York City. We turned up the TV and leaned in to watch the first images of the US Airways "Miracle on the Hudson" flight floating down the frozen river. No sooner had those first horrifying pictures splashed across the screen, than the doctor came into the room, ashen-faced and grave with his findings. My mother had lung cancer, which he estimated to be stage 3. Optimistically, he thought she might see another year of life, two at best. I was gutted by the unexpected news that hit me like a runaway car careening through an intersection.

Back in New York, I met with my supervisor and applied for a hardship transfer to the Long Beach crew base. On my application, I explained that my mom was starting chemotherapy and that I would be my mother's primary caregiver. My supervisor was sympathetic and encouraged my plans to move to California at once. I flew back West and took up residence in my mother's guest bedroom.

While on reserve status with the airline in New York, I was required to call in the morning to receive my assignment for the day ahead. During the confusion of the move, I missed an assigned call-in window and received a written disciplinary warning, unexplainably skipping the customary verbal warning. This would prove catastrophic in the months to come.

Shortly after my move back to California, I logged on to the company website to select my schedule for the following month. To my surprise, the computer indicated that I was still based at JFK. I called my supervisor back in New York who told me that my base award had been rescinded and that he had simply forgotten to notify me. His solution was that I could simply commute each week to JFK to sit reserve. I explained that this was virtually impossible as my mother was about to begin chemotherapy.

The company offered a compromise of a 30-day unpaid leave of absence beginning May 1ˢᵗ during which I could "settle my affairs" and then I would need to return to flying my reserve schedule out of New York. I was livid.

My mother insisted that Ken and I take the cruise before she started chemotherapy and I reluctantly agreed to do so. I finished my month of flying at JFK on the 25ᵗʰ of April and Ken and I flew to Fort Lauderdale and boarded the ship for seven days R&R in the Western Caribbean.

Upon our return to Fort Lauderdale, we proceeded to the JetBlue ticket counter to check in for our flights back to New York for Ken, and to Los Angeles for me. The agent looked grim as she clicked away at the computer, attempting to process our standby tickets. She sighed, looked at me, and then told me that because I was on a personal leave, my travel privileges had been suspended. I felt like I had been punched in the stomach. I felt humiliated standing there in front of my boyfriend feeling betrayed by my company, not knowing how I was going to get him back to work in New York the next morning. Nor did I know how I was going to get myself out to California to care for my mother.

I walked over to the US Airways counter on the verge of tears. The agent was horrified by my story and before I knew it, we were headed down the concourse with two full-fare tickets to JFK and a flight for me out to Burbank in the morning.

Back home in California two weeks later and just in from taking my mom to chemotherapy, I received a phone call from my supervisor demanding that I return to New York for a disciplinary hearing. When I asked what it was in reference to, I was told I would be informed at the meeting. This, of course, required another ticket purchase on US

Airways as my travel privileges on my own airline were still suspended.

Back in New York, I was escorted into a conference room where several supervisors and a human resources manager I'd never seen before were already seated around a conference table. I felt ambushed and betrayed. Once seated, my supervisor informed me in a snide tone of voice that I had been given a leave of absence to take care of my "dying mother," not to take a cruise with my boyfriend.

I was then placed on a two-week suspension pending termination review. I was stunned. The cruise had begun during the month of April, before the leave, and returned on the 3rd of May. And furthermore, of what business was it of the company's what I did on my personal time? No one had ever stipulated what I was and was not permitted to do with the awarded time off. The company had far overstepped.

Over the next few months, flight attendants junior to me were awarded transfers to the Long Beach base. When I brought this to management's attention, I was told that due to that first written disciplinary action, I had been barred from transferring for six months and thus been passed over when transfers had been awarded. JetBlue personnel "guidelines" called for six steps of "progressive guidance" beginning with a verbal warning between a first infraction and "termination review." Yet, I had received a written warning for my first missed call-in window, thus rendering me ineligible for transfer when the vacancy became available. And with the impromptu command performance at JFK, I skipped another three levels of prescribed discipline to arrive at "Termination Review." When I brought up the arbitrary nature of my disciplinary proceedings, my supervisor told me I should be grateful I had a job because a lot of former TWA people weren't so lucky, and that the company was doing me a favor by keeping me on. In a past personal conversation, I had confided that I was an alcoholic in recovery. Now, I was also told that I should be thankful the company was willing to take a chance on me as such.

Without union representation or a contract to bind the company to adhere to its own policies and procedures, there was nothing to keep the management from proceeding in its arbitrary and capricious whims.

I was totally at the mercy of disinterested and disingenuous managers who seemingly wanted me gone.

My next avenue of recourse was to file for FMLA. At this time, I was serving as the Chairman of the Uniform Redesign Committee and I had been elected to the Quality of Work Life team from among 1,400 JFK-based crewmembers, tackling scheduling, benefits, and labor relations issues. This work required me to occasionally drop trips to work at corporate headquarters alongside company executives or in the field. When I submitted an application for FMLA leave, it was denied. I was told that the company would only recognize actual flight hours, not the total hours in service to the company. When my committee and headquarters hours were factored in, I was well in excess of the minimum threshold. The company refused to budge and I was forced to continue to commute. JetBlue has since been heavily penalized by the State of New York for violating employees' access to FMLA and for unfairly penalizing employees exercising their sick leave rights. But none of this helped me in 2010.

As my mother's condition deteriorated, the juggling act that was caretaking, commuting cross-country, and flying my monthly schedule become vexing. I often woke up with the California sunrise and began the long and painstaking task of getting my mother up and dressed, and into the car for chemotherapy. I would then do the grocery shopping and laundry and handle the seemingly endless phone calls that a terminal illness requires. Later, I would bring her home and make her relatively comfortable until the caregiver arrived. I would then race around the house throwing my belongings into my suitcase and beg a friend to drive me to the airport an hour away where I would stand by for an overbooked flight to JFK. Once onboard, I would rest for a few hours, often landing just before sunrise. Many times, a flight assignment awaited my arrival and I would run straight to the gate and work a full flight to the Caribbean and back before I could head home and collapse into bed.

These days of emotionally laden caretaking and arduous transcontinental commutes, followed by long days of flying, left me physically and emotionally spent. No longer was there time for AA meetings or visits with my psychiatrist. Soon, the occasional glass of wine with my First Class meal on my commute started to look appealing again, just one to take the edge off. I was stressed out and exhausted and Lord knew, I had earned it. I began to accept invitations to join my crew for "debriefings," informal gatherings in the hotel bar after a long day of flying. By the summer of 2010, I was not only joining my crew for happy hour, but I was returning to my room to do some heavy drinking alone afterwards. I was right back to full-on alcoholic binge drinking.

My glamorous mother

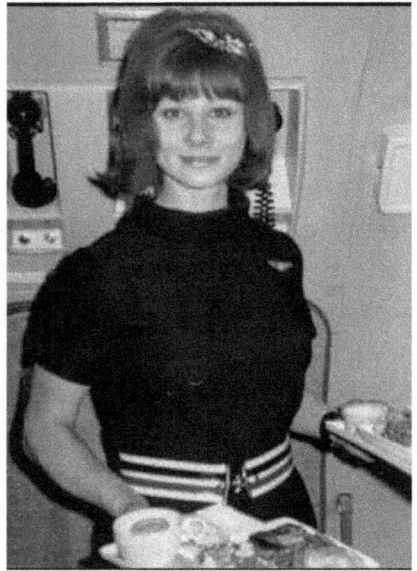
My mom, the quintessential
'60's stewardess

Aviation runs in my blood

I have always loved a uniform

Honolulu- bound with my dad in a 747, 1983

19 years old, fresh faced and wide- eyed: Salt Lake to Billings with
SkyWest, 1991

On the interview circuit, 2010

Business Express Airlines, Boston, 1994

First Class with Delta, Salt Lake City to JFK, 1998

Back in the skies with JetBlue, 2008

Fun at JFK, 2009

CHAPTER 10

My crew and I arrived at the hotel in Portland, Maine on the afternoon of August 8, 2010, and made plans to meet for dinner. I was flying with an old friend, a former colleague from another airline who I hadn't seen in years. The cockpit crew was great fun and the four of us had hit it off instantly when we began the trip a day earlier at JFK. That night, we explored the old Wharf District and had a delicious seafood dinner and a lot of laughs. On the way back to the hotel, we stopped into a divey pool hall and shot a few rounds. We did a lot of drinking as well. It was great fun, and one of the most enjoyable layovers I had in years.

Back at the hotel, I ran into a flying friend and a couple crew members from another base and joined them in the lobby for a nightcap and a few more laughs. It was a grand time. The night stretched into the pre-dawn and soon I realized pickup was in just a couple hours. At length, I excused myself and staggered up to my room. I had definitely overdone it and I laid on my bed as the room began to spin. I closed my eyes for a short time then pulled myself together and headed downstairs to meet my crew for the short ride to the airport.

We rode out to the airport with a fun Delta crew and laughed the whole way as a light rain fell. The first leg of the day was a quick hop down to JFK with a half-full airplane. After the service, I sat on the jumpseat in the darkened cabin with a cup of coffee, nursing a hangover. We changed planes at JFK and I ran into a few friends on the concourse and we exchanged hugs and promises to catch up soon.

All that remained was a quick Pittsburgh turnaround and we would be back by noon. Pittsburgh had always been one of my favorite cities to fly to. Courteous, low-maintenance passengers, and a lot of off-duty, commuting airline personnel made it one of the easiest flights in the system. We took off with a full load and I was looking forward to the quick return flight and my 20 days off at the end of the trip.

Twelve life vests dislodged from beneath the seats and flew out into the aisle when the captain hit the brakes on the runway at the Greater Pittsburgh International Airport. As this was a known safety issue with our E-190 aircraft and a committee had been working on this very issue, this infuriated me. Less than a year ago, the world had watched the brilliant evacuation of US Airways flight 1549 on the Hudson River. Had one of our aircraft suffered the same fate, we would have had a far different, tragic outcome. One of the company's "core values" was safety. Yet our esteemed management could not be bothered to ameliorate this issue despite the tireless work on behalf of this concern.

I began to grow angry, thinking about this egregious negligence as well as the hypocrisy with which a company whose core values—safety, caring, integrity, passion, and fun—had dropped me on my ass in my time of need with my mother's illness. I began to boil. In addition to the residual alcohol in my bloodstream and the psychiatric medication missing from it, the fuse had been lit for a spectacular flashpoint.

On my knees restowing the scattered life vests that had been flung about the cabin, I felt a searing rage wash across my body. I felt degraded and abused. I was still on the floor when the first passengers began to trickle through the boarding door which only served to piss me off further. I sprung up and headed toward the forward galley to greet the incoming customers while tucking in my shirt and dusting off my knees.

Only a handful of passengers had straggled aboard when I noticed a woman struggling to fit a rolling bag into the overhead compartment above row 6 or 7. I sighed with annoyance and stepped into the aisle and approached to offer assistance.

What happened next was quick and sudden and left me reeling. One moment I was reaching up to assist with the luggage, suggesting we turn it sideways then suddenly, I was knocked back into the row adjacent having been hit hard in the forehead by the bag. There was a sharp crack of pain and everything went dark for a moment as my eyes filled with tears. Instinctively, I put my hand to my forehead and when I pulled it away, there was blood on my palm.

I started quickly up the aisle to survey myself in the lavatory mirror. At row 2, a woman stopped me and said something about a spill. I snapped that I needed to take care of myself first and that I would be back. After the flight, this passenger would go on television complaining in a nasally whine about how incredibly "rude, ruder than one expects from the 'service on an airline'" I was for not stopping then and there to deal with her concern.

I stepped into the lavatory and locked the door behind me. I stood shaking with rage, steadying myself on the countertop and looked myself in the eye in the mirror. Suddenly, I realized that this was no longer the job I once loved. Blood had been drawn. A line had been crossed. I knew then that I was done.

When I came out of the lavatory, the captain was turned around in his seat and asked what had occurred. When I told him, he asked if I wanted the passenger removed. I was livid but replied, "No, we're full and I have a jumpseater. It's only an hour. How bad can it be?" Besides. I was to be off for the next 20 days and had designs on a First Class seat on a United Airlines nonstop to LAX departing shortly after our arrival. And on some level, I knew I wouldn't be doing this again.

Boarding was a disaster with dozens of oversized bags lugged aboard by an unusually uncooperative and entitled crowd. I was frustrated by both the number of unwieldy carry-ons parading down the jetway and by the unwillingness of several cantankerous and crotchety passengers to part with their precious possessions.

Now enraged by the insult of physical injury upon my already agitated state, I dropped all pretense of hospitality and focused solely on compliance and getting the boarding door closed as quickly as possible in an effort to propel myself toward my days off and as far away from this abhorrent job as possible.

Emotional regulation can be daunting for the untreated bipolar. With nothing to buffer the everyday mood swings that everyone experiences, the bipolar can lurch into uncontrollable and frightening extremes of emotion. Anger can feel like racing down the freeway with no brakes.

By now, I had long passed the point of no return, and was just along for the ride, although I was as of yet unaware of what was transpiring. I had crossed a line into a powerful mania, my rage fueled by potent chemical reactions and ratcheting up toward an inexorable crescendo.

I spent much of the flight contemplating my disenchantment. I thought about my mother, dying back home in California, and I began to re-evaluate my priorities. The job was standing in my way of taking care of her, there was no doubt about it. I was exhausted. I was furious and resentful at my company for putting me in this position. I admitted to myself for the first time that I didn't want to do this anymore. I could afford to quit, I had the savings to take a year or so off. Of course, resigning would mean the end of my travel benefits but this really wasn't the time to be gallivanting around the world, anyhow. I had enjoyed a fabulous career and had the time of my life with no regrets. At length, I decided I would resign upon arrival in New York, effective immediately. With that decision came an enormous sense of relief. It was as if a great sodden blanket had been lifted from my back.

Seated on my jumpseat, I took in a deep breath and looked around the cabin. Bright sunshine streamed through the windows. Most of the passengers were staring intently into the screens of their seat-back televisions—at least the screens that actually worked. Some were reading. Few had bothered with the simple common courtesies of "Please" or "Thank you" a few minutes earlier when I served their beverages. In fact, more than one hadn't even looked up when spoken to. I wouldn't miss this, I thought to myself. It had been fun once, but it no longer held allure.

This impending liberation called for celebration, and I stepped into the galley where I discreetly poured myself a vodka tonic in a paper coffee cup, then returned to the jumpseat where I sat sipping defiantly, simply passing time until New York and my emancipation. A second cocktail brought on a sense of hope and mischievousness and I began to grow excited for my new and shining future, free of the shitshow that was JetBlue Airways and the inglorious heathen otherwise known as the traveling public. Descent came quickly and I made a half-hearted pass through the cabin collecting service items in a plastic bag and brusquely instructing passengers to fasten their seatbelts. Toward the back of the aircraft, I instructed a man to raise his seat back. Passing the row behind him, I caught him recline the seat once more as I walked away. I turned back and slapped the back of his seat hard, launching him forward in his seat, startling him and causing him to gasp, his eyes wide. He would recount this experience on a morning talk show the next day. I was truly out of fucks to give on Flight 1052.

The aircraft turned off the runway at JFK and I made some tersely worded "Welcome to New York" announcement. By now I was feeling no pain. It was a bright and beautiful, sun-drenched day and I was debating heading home to the beach house and enjoying an afternoon on the sand and proceeding to Los Angeles in the morning. Besides, once I quit, I would no longer be able to passride on United and I would have to buy a ticket before I could travel in the morning. These were the thoughts that were rambling through my head when the aircraft pulled up to gate 15 at Terminal 5 and the fasten seatbelt sign was turned out.

I rose from my jumpseat and "disarmed" my door by operating a lever that detached the emergency escape slide from the door so that the passengers could disembark freely. I then crossed over and into the forward galley where I repeated the procedure at the galley service door. The main cabin door was then opened and the first few passengers began to deplane. "Bags on 3!" yelled the agent from halfway up the jet bridge.

Standing at the forward entrance door, I picked up the intercom handset, prepared to say, "Ladies and gentlemen, if you've checked luggage aboard today's flight, it can be collected at carousel number 3."

Suddenly the woman from row 7 appeared before me, nostrils flared, all snort and huff. "Where's my bag, motherfucker?" she hissed, low and seething, eyes boring into mine.

What happened then can only be described as an out-of-body experience. I was only vaguely aware of raising the handset back to my mouth. I have only the slightest recollection of depressing the PA button and I only know what I said through piecing together various media and witness reports. Evidently what came out of my mouth was not directions to baggage claim but rather the following statement:

"Ladies and gentlemen:

To those of you on today's flight who have showed us dignity and respect, I thank you.

But to the bitch who just called me a motherfucker, FUCK you.

I have had 20 years of this shit and I'm out."

I felt that familiar zap of electricity jolt through my brain as I took leave of my body in much the same way I did when I slammed my car into another years earlier. The most delicious, euphoric elation washed over me and I was consumed by a sense of invincibility and superhuman strength. Mania is far more exquisite than any drug and I was now riding high, in full flight from reality.

I concluded decisively that I was done with the job then and there. I extended my palm out in a universal stop sign to halt traffic in the aisle and stomped to row 1 where my rolling suitcase and tote sat in the overhead compartment. I flung my luggage down into the aisle and began to strap it all together while my startled passengers stood watching, aghast.

I intended to simply walk off the aircraft, down to operations, and throw my wings and ID badge on my supervisor's desk and thank him for the ride. Then it occurred to me that I had put in 20 years into the industry and was walking away with absolutely nothing to show for it. I decided the least this shittin' company could do was give me one for the road. I wheeled my luggage into the galley, placed my tote bag on the galley counter, and unzipped it. Then I ripped open the bar cart and pulled out the liquor kit which contained 77 miniature bottles of booze. I quickly dumped the entire contents into my tote bag, then slammed the empty drawer back into the cart, closed the door, and resealed the cart carefully. I zipped my tote bag back up and attached it to my suitcase with the nylon strap.

As I stood back up, I glanced outside through the tiny porthole in the door. The day was resplendent. Warm, bright light bathed the tarmac below and I felt the sun's warmth just outside. Instinctively, I felt an urgent need to be out of the aircraft and in that basking light.

More so, I felt a compelling need to be heard. I felt a need for justice. I knew my departure from the company would not even register on the dispassioned, corporate radar. I needed to know that a serious self-appraisal would be conducted by the company so that perhaps others behind me would not be abused the way I had been. My departure had to get their attention. Yet, there was no premeditation on what that might look like. In my manic state, thoughts were flying at me with such velocity that there was no time to filter them for logic.

As if on automatic pilot, I took a good look out the window, assessing the outside conditions, as flight attendants are trained to do, and even laughed at myself, dismissing what I was doing in its incongruity to the moment. Then suddenly and inexplicably, I was shaking and reaching out for the lever that armed the slide. With a resounding thud, I slammed it down into the "armed" position and without hesitation, I grasped firmly the door opening lever and jammed it up into the "open" position even as one of the pilots was approaching from behind imploring me not to do so. There was a brief discussion but in the adrenaline surge, it was as if I were in a tunnel with everything around me an indecipherable din. Words tumbled from my mouth an unformed gibberish.

There was the sound of a muffled but profound explosion and the aircraft swayed to and fro and I had to hang on to the doorframe as the aircraft pitched up. The raw power of the slide inflating was awe-inspiring. In mere seconds, the slide had folded out and extended, slapping the concrete below with great force, stirring up a cloud of dust and debris on all sides. Suddenly, I was blinded by the bright light from outside as I stood there blinking in the blinding sunshine. My ears rang with the whine of passing jet engines and the clang of baggage carts passing by on the ramp.

Once I regained my composure, my first impression was how incredibly steep and high the slide was compared to the cabin simulators I had trained on and I thought to myself that there was no way to get down this thing without sustaining injury. I realized, however, that there was no time to delay and no going back now. I grabbed the handle of my suitcase with my left hand and crouched down to squeeze through the low door frame, then I leapt into the glorious, enveloping sunshine.

In that first second, which seemed to stretch forever as I hovered weightless outside the aircraft, I felt a delicious, blissful abandon. I experienced an indescribable sense of liberation and escape. Within seconds, I bounced down onto the slide like a kid in a funhouse and laughed uproariously as I picked up speed, exhilarated, racing toward emancipation and liberty and the sundrenched tarmac below. In a flash, I landed flat on my ass on the hot pavement, howling with laughter and missing a shoe as the baggage handlers gathered around laughing in amazement.

I righted myself, found my shoe a few feet away, and then realized my baggage was still up in the aircraft. This presented a real dilemma. I knew I couldn't exactly walk up the jetway stairs, knock on the door, and ask for my luggage. I realized I was going to have to get back up into the aircraft 15 feet off the tarmac somehow via the escape slide and retrieve my luggage. This was most critical, given the fact that it contained a stolen liquor kit, as if that were the worst of my problems at this point.

I threw myself face-down on the narrow slide and wrapped my

arms around the bolstered sides. With great effort, I got a tenuous grip on one side of the slide and climbed up a few feet before slipping and sliding back down to the ground. On my third try, I was able to shimmy up just high enough to reach up and grab the handle of my luggage which lay on its side on the galley floor protruding slightly out the open door. I went sliding back down now for a second time, on my face this time with 50 pounds of luggage and a stolen liquor kit which came crashing down on top of my head. This was a far less elegant landing than the first time, scoring me no points. I stood up and strapped my luggage together, waved to the ramp agents, and walked across the tarmac to the terminal. After trying a few doors, I found one which led into the bowels of the terminal and headed for the parking lot, thrilled to put the ordeal of JetBlue Airways behind me forever.

My heart pounded as I pulled my wheeled suitcase through the maze of underground corridors toward the baggage claim, sporting a broad, deranged smile. The few coworkers I passed seemed oblivious to my presence despite the bloody gash across my forehead and word had not yet spread of my audacious departure. I scurried past the employee cafeteria and quickly exited a door into the buzz of the baggage claim. I glided between the carousels unnoticed. I mounted the escalator to the ticketing level and the AirTrain which would whisk me to the parking lot. As I ascended above the pandemonium of the ticketing level and its snarling and snaking security line, I thought gleefully that I would never have to navigate that fiasco again.

Suddenly, a man's voice called out excitedly from behind, "Hey, weren't you the steward on the flight from Pittsburgh?" I turned to face a smiling businessman smiling excitedly. "Dude! Did you just quit? That was awesome!" the man fawned. I tugged my tie off from around my neck, pulled my ID and lanyard over my head, and flung them both deep into the teeming crowd of the ticketing lobby below, laughing heartily.

CHAPTER 11

The squeal of my tires skidding into the driveway took Ken by surprise. "GODDAMN YOU, YOU'RE DRUNK!" shrieked Ken as I careened into the living room after rebounding off the entryway walls.

"But I have something wonderful to tell you!" I exclaimed. Ken was stricken and the look of fear on his face as he sat holding his breath beside me on our seafoam green Ikea sofa was more than I could take. I burst out laughing. I folded my hands in my lap and started again. "Okay, you know those weekend trips we like to take to Florida? Well, we're going to have to find a travel agent who can us get us some good deals." I paused to let that sink in.

Anger flashed over his face and he sat up stiffly. "You did NOT quit that job. No, you did NOT."

I quickly launched into a rapid-fire dissertation reminding him how poorly the airline had treated me. I said I could afford to take time off and I told him I had savings he didn't know anything about. I promised nothing would change despite this development. I was talking a mile a minute doing damage control.

Ken put out his hands for me to stop. "I can NOT deal with you," he seethed through clenched teeth. "I have to lay down." He stood up and walked out of the room and down the hallway, slamming the bedroom door behind him and leaving me to gaze out at the ocean wondering if it was something I said.

Not daring to disturb him, I opened my suitcase and took out a pair of faded Madras shorts and an oversized olive green t-shirt and slipped them on in the living room then poured myself a cocktail in a coffee mug. I dialed my mother in California. She thought my story was hysterical and we were both in stitches when there came a knock at the door. By now, I was hammered. I figured it was my neighbor, Jeanne, who often stopped by for a cup of coffee after one of my trips. I told my mom I would call her back, hung up, and rose to answer the door.

I swung the door open to face not my neighbor but two square-jawed, stone-faced detectives in well-tailored suits. My eyes were immediately drawn beyond them to the sight of two unmarked cars blocking my driveway and a dozen or so New York Port Authority police cars lined up to the end of the block, their blue and red lights flashing garishly, lighting up the facades of the houses down the street. Startled neighbors huddled in small groups on the sidewalk, gazing upon the extravaganza. Overhead, three helicopters hovered noisily.

The two men introduced themselves as detectives with the New York Port Authority Police and asked me if I was indeed Steven Slater, JetBlue flight attendant, and if I had worked Flight 1052 into JFK that afternoon. They asked if I had deployed an emergency escape slide and I answered in the affirmative. They then informed me that I was under arrest and would be transported back to JFK for questioning. I took another look around at the spectacle of the police cars, the helicopters, the nosy neighbors, and the Columbo twins on my front porch and got a case of the giggles that I could not stifle despite the gravity of the situation.

Blown slides are a fact of life at every airline. In my last year at Delta, there had been 27 inadvertent slide deployments. At no time had I considered what I had done in any way illegal. I knew I would have an internal issue with my ex-employer, but at no point did it ever occur to me that there could be legal ramifications to my little stunt. This all seemed so ridiculous and unnecessary. If they wanted to talk about this they simply could have called me and I would have driven back to the airport. There was no need for this over-the-top, heavy-handed shitshow.

The detectives read me my Miranda rights. I was instructed to turn around and was promptly handcuffed. The officers looked at my bare feet and asked if there was anyone in the house to bring me a pair of shoes. I replied that my partner was in the bedroom. One of the detectives bellowed his name and suddenly Kenneth appeared at the bedroom door, startled and disoriented, in a pair of blue silk boxers. The detectives explained that I was under arrest and headed back to the airport as Ken scurried to grab a pair of shoes from the bedroom and slip them on my feet. When the story broke the next day, it was reported that I was in the throes of passion with my gay lover when the police arrived at my home.

I was placed in the back of one of the unmarked police cars and we sped down Cross Bay Boulevard back to the airport and the compact and efficient Port Authority Police station on the south side of the airfield. I was led into the precinct and sat down at a desk to be interrogated. Wildly intoxicated, I could not keep my story straight. I couldn't remember much of the flight, nor the sequence of events. Still insanely manic, I kept breaking into fits of giggles and inappropriate laughter over the most random of minutiae. The detectives were amused by the story and found it highly entertaining. It seemed everybody had had enough of entitled and high-strung passengers and off the record, nobody could really blame me for my outburst. On the record, however, I was in a lot of hot water. I was to be arraigned in Queen's Supreme Court in the morning on charges of Criminal Mischief, Reckless Endangerment, and Criminal Trespass—and would spend the night in a cell.

My cell was a small and blindingly white affair lit by garish fluorescent lights with a concrete slab for a bed and a silver metal toilet behind a low-slung cinder block wall. For the first half of the evening, I shared it with a scruffy Middle Eastern taxi driver who had been picked up for cruising the terminal roadway with no medallion. An icy blast of Arctic air blew down upon me from a vent in the ceiling causing me to shiver beneath a gauzy paper blanket.

Later that day I was visited by my legal aid attorney, Howard Turman, a mild-mannered, jovial man who also happened to be blind. Howard explained the gravity of the charges. I was looking at up to seven years behind bars. This news made my head spin. Seven years for a slide deployment was truly absurd. Howard explained the next steps, and the arraignment procedures I would face the next morning in court. I laid back down beneath my paper blanket and sobered up quickly.

The next morning, I was led to an unmarked car in the parking lot to be transferred to Queens Supreme Court for my arraignment. Walking out of the station house and across the parking lot, we were ambushed by two reporters and a couple of photographers with long lens cameras. Ever the people- pleasing flight attendant, I felt it my duty to smile for the photographers.

"Mr. Slater, why are you smiling?" shouted one of the reporters. "Why are you smiling?" "What do you have to say, Mr. Slater?" the reporters yelled as I grinned broadly. I knew nothing about the press. I did not know that this would cause me to appear cocky to the public and the courts.

"I hate fucking reporters," said one of the policemen as we pulled out of the parking lot and onto the airport roadway. Pulling into the courthouse on Queens Boulevard, we were approached by even more photographers and reporters. Again, I smiled warmly and answered questions, appearing to enjoy this new media spotlight like some attention-seeking starlet. I was only trying to be helpful and not to appear aloof.

The wood-paneled, august courtroom was teaming with defendants, attorneys, and spectators. Ken was already seated in the gallery and had taken notice of a large contingent of reporters gathered to report on my arraignment. The room was a flourish of activity as defendants were ushered in and out in rapid succession. I was brought before the judge and called to the stand, Howard Turman at my side, where I stood incredulous as I listened to the charges levied against me. I was unable to comprehend how something so innocuous had turned into a high crime. I pled not guilty. Bail was set at $2,500.

I was quickly ushered out a side entrance and shackled to another prisoner, then boarded onto an ominous, black and white Corrections bus with bars on the windows. I was seated in the front row with two hulking corrections officers ensconced on the bench seat opposite us. In front of us, sat another row of formidable officers and ahead, the driver sat in a steel-barred cage. Heavy gauge bars across the windows all but precluded outside visibility and the interior was lit by overhead lights down the aisle. Around 3:30, we set sail for the long and tedious rush hour crawl up the Van Wyck Expressway to the Vernon C. Bain Correctional Center in the Bronx.

"The Boat," a massive and looming floating prison complex, is a 625-foot-long by 125-foot-wide flatbed barge with 14 dormitories and 100 cells for inmates anchored off the South Bronx, and is used as a processing center for incoming prisoners headed to Rikers Island. Surrounded by high fences and barbed wire, it cuts the imposing path of a maximum security facility. By now, word of my airport adventure had passed through the law enforcement and corrections community. I received a very warm and enthusiastic, if not disarming, welcome from the corrections and administration staff, and was asked to tell my story time and again to applause and cheers.

Two stern and heavyset female corrections agents pulled me aside and asked me if I knew just where I was and exactly what I was up against. Did I understand just how much danger I was in? they prodded. When I replied that I was basically lost and in over my head, they laid it out for me. This was Rikers Island. The big time. I was basically entering Oz. They told me to brace myself for a lot of overt racism, homophobia, and brutal violence, and explained that I would be an easy target. My head spun. Who would want to hurt me? I had nothing against anyone. They advised me to feign illness immediately, and to mention my HIV status before I even finished processing. That would land me in sick bay, and hopefully buy a long enough delay for my bail to be posted so that I might be released before I had to enter general population, if at all. At worst, it would grant me housing in a different and safer population if I had to stay any length of time. They were insistent that I was in grave danger and must follow their instructions to the letter. For the first time since the big jump I began to feel fear.

I was led to a single cell where I was placed for my own protection. Exhausted from the 24-hour adrenaline rush and the lack of sleep, I fell quickly into a deep slumber.

"SLATER!" one of the guards was suddenly calling to me. "You're famous, bro!" I sat up and rubbed my eyes in the bright overhead light, baffled. Just outside the bars of my cell, the young Italian cop fanned out two newspapers with a broad grin on his face. "You're a big hero now, man. This fuckin' city loves you. You're on every TV station and all over the radio. Check these out, bro." I walked over to the bars and blinked repeatedly as my face stared back from the *New York Post* and the *Daily News* he held in his hands with the headlines, "Plainly Nuts" and "Freakin Flier" splashed across the front page. I was stunned. This was surreal and absurd. Nothing made sense.

By the time I was led to an open holding cell to join a dozen other inmates for a cheese sandwich and a glass of milk, an excited buzz had descended upon the processing center, with incoming prisoners recognizing me and the next shift of curious wardens peppering me with questions. I was suddenly an accidental celebrity, receiving cheers and ovations everywhere I went. The corrections officers were particularly big fans, telling me I had lived out a fantasy that everyone could appreciate.

While I sat formulating my survival plan, Ken repositioned himself to the home of my friend Taryn, an urbane and elegant career woman who lived in an opulent yet homey penthouse apartment in a stately pre-war building off Park Avenue. Together, they had gone to work sourcing my bail and fielding numerous inquiries from an increasingly intrusive press.

Later in the evening, I was pulled aside by one of the wardens who told me that although Ken was working on my bail and I could be out in a few hours, a major news outlet was offering to post my bail at that moment in exchange for the exclusive to my story. He strongly recommended I take the deal, averting a night in jail. I said I needed to talk to Ken and against regulations, he put me on the phone with him. After a lengthy discussion, I decided it was too risky a commitment. I was facing felony criminal charges and couldn't risk saying something in an interview that could potentially incriminate me and sabotage my freedom. The guards were shocked by my risky decision but I stood steadfast. When my bail came through in the later hours, the prison administration faced a new dilemma. They had never faced a media event of this magnitude and did not know how to guarantee a safe release. In fact, camera trucks clogged the front gate making exit near impossible.

A plan was devised to announce that I was exiting the front gate and transported back to Belle Harbor in a police vehicle when instead, an officer would shepherd me into an awaiting taxi parked off to the side and I would be driven to Taryn's penthouse in Manhattan.

When the appointed hour arrived, I was escorted to the side entrance and my handcuffs unlocked. The door was swung open and suddenly I faced a vast sea of angry, dazzling floodlights and microphones as fifty reporters descended ravenously upon me. I was instantly blinded by the sulphurous explosion of high-watt paparazzi flashbulbs. Still, I strode out confidently, a broad smile on my face, again believing I needed to "Sparkle Neely, Sparkle." These people had showed up in the late night hours to see me. I felt a moral obligation to charm and entertain. I did not understand that this was simply their job, and yet I put my best foot forward to make them comfortable, just as I would have on the airplane. This worked to my advantage, as I was seen as a good sport and a wry and ironic knucklehead who could laugh at himself. I made friends with the media that night and showed myself a good sport. I knew nothing of the delicate, codependent and symbiotic dance that is media fame. I would get my crash course in the days to come and prove a formidable apprentice.

In the blinding glare and deafening screech of the frenzied tumult, I was swallowed, surrounded, and suffocated by the teaming mob of shouting reporters each yelling over the other. The crowd ahead gave me no more than a foot to move forward. I began to panic and hyperventilate as rapid fire questions volleyed and lobbied overhead. Still, I kept a perfect flight attendant smile on my face.

Suddenly, a figure in black jumped into my blurry vision. I drew a sharp, startled breathed then let out a sigh of relief with the recollection that I was to be escorted to the taxi by a uniformed officer. "Take my hand," a solid and steady man's voice implored over the din. Instinctively, I reached for his and we set off at a dead run, busting away from the throng of reporters and cameramen weighed down by their heavy equipment and the coiffed reporters tethered by their microphones on cumbersome cords. I broke out in laughter from the adventure and sport of the moment, feeling victorious at having left my tormentors in the dust.

We quickly approached a silver minivan. The door slid open, and we jumped inside, the man in black first, and I next to him on the bench seat. Suddenly the door slammed shut and someone behind me reached over my shoulder and locked the door. With a sinking feeling, I realized immediately that something was very wrong. At once, a fourth person seated behind yelled, "GO! GO! GO!" as the vehicle started to speed away and down the front driveway of the jail, then turned on to a dark and unfamiliar Bronx street.

Suddenly, a well-dressed man turned around in the front passenger seat and smiled at me. "Hello, Steven! I'm Bruce Johnston, Senior News Editor with ABC News. We'd love to talk to you about your amazing story! Would you be willing to give us an exclusive interview?" Bruce Johnston smiled broadly and warmly, handing me a business card. I was repulsed and enraged. I looked around the vehicle at all the fresh network faces smiling expectantly. I looked at the slight and balding young man sitting in the seat beside me who I had mistaken for a cop. For a brief second, I thought about punching him in the mouth. I turned back to the editor and hissed, "Did you just kidnap me on live TV? There must be 100 reporters back there and the whole world just saw this happen. Take. Me. Back. NOW!" I spat. Incredulously, I was now asking to be returned to jail, willfully.

Pulling back up to Vernon Bain, I stepped from the minivan to find that only two reporters and their cameramen remained. They ran over to me at once. "Whaddya doin' back, Steven?" a male reporter in a chambray shirt asked.

I shrugged and quipped, "The food was just too good." Then I walked up to the guard shack, explained what had just happened, and asked him to call me a cab.

Once ensconced in the back seat, we proceeded toward the city. "Who are these people following us?" the Indian cab driver asked nervously a few blocks away. "I do not like this." I turned around to see four news vans following us closely down the otherwise deserted night streets.

"Fuck," I said to myself.

"WHAT DID YOU DO?" wailed the driver, staring at me in the rearview mirror with wide eyes. He made numerous sweeping, broad turns down the quiet, residential streets then pulled over. After a moment, the driver asked in a timid voice, "Excuse me, Sir, do you know where we are?" He then made a phone call in agitated and aggrieved Hindi, looking at the camera crews in the rearview mirror and gesturing wildly. For a terrifying moment, I thought he was going to call the ride off and dump me there on the curb. Finally, he got back on the road and proceeded toward the city, driving increasingly faster, trying to lose the dogged camera trucks until we were racing through the Queens Midtown Tunnel at high speed, visions of Princess Diana dancing in my head.

"THEY ARE STILL HERE!" the driver squealed in panic as he screeched to a stop in front of Taryn's building on East 67th Street. The taxi was nose-to-nose with two more TV vans that had somehow joined the pursuit in addition to the four that now pulled up to the curb from behind. I jumped out and ran into the building leaving the doorman to pay the taxi. I sprinted into the waiting elevator and rode up to the penthouse where I flew into Ken's waiting arms.

Within minutes, the street below was swarmed with reporters and camera crews. We rode out a sleepless night in relative peace in the insulated quiet of the penthouse high above the city, a world removed from the din and chaos below. By now, my story was on every channel and I sat in disbelief as my face flashed across the screen in Tanya's sumptuous living room. I called my mother in California to check in and made a few calls to worried friends and coworkers. No one could believe the media pandemonium that had ensued since my arrest and everyone was deeply concerned for my well-being and safety.

Early the next morning, a woman knocked on the door and introduced herself as a reporter for the *New York Times* who just happened to also live in the building. We exchanged pleasantries and I excused myself and closed the door. A bit later, I started out for the office of my bail bondsman. I rode the elevator down to the lobby with this woman and a cameraman who had been waiting in the hallway for me to exit the apartment and made the mistake of engaging in casual conversation. Again being media naive, I thought nothing of it. I did not realize that I was being filmed as we spoke. The reporter asked if going down the slide was something I had thought about doing. I replied, "Yes, I have thought about this moment for 20 years," referring to my years of annual recurrent training preparing for an emergency evacuation. "It's something you often think about doing but you never think it will actually happen," I added.

The elevator doors opened into the lobby and I stepped out into a sea of reporters who mobbed and followed me to the bail bondsman's office much the way they had when I was released from Vernon Bain. That afternoon, the *New York Times* ran a headline, "Flight attendant had long imagined escaping down the emergency chute" along with excerpts of the conversation in the elevator which they were now billing as an "exclusive interview." I was livid. Online, they ran the surreptitious footage. I knew I could not go back to Taryn's apartment, as it would be unfair to subject her to further intrusion, so Ken and I proceeded back to our home in Belle Harbor, followed all the way by a horde of reporters.

For the next 24 hours, we were held captives in our home with six or seven media vans parked in front of the house at all times. Every hour on the hour, bright flood lights illuminated our windows as reporters gave live reports from my doorstep. Ironically, I did not own a television and was unable to see these "Breaking News" reports. I could not open my door for the crush of shouting reporters who would push their way inside my home shoving microphones in my face. Neighbors and flight attendant friends fought their way through the clamoring mob and brought meals and the latest news to my side door. We were truly under siege.

By now the network's quest for the "Steven Slater Interview" had reached a fevered pitch with every media outlet clamoring for access. My phone rang incessantly with callers ranging from local television reporters to the biggest names in primetime news. Hearing the voice of Katie Couric or Jane Pauley speaking to me personally from my answering machine was surreal. One message might be from the producer of *60 Minutes,* and the next might be from George Stephanopoulos himself. I dared not answer the phone but rather sat, mouth agape in shock, paralyzed and staring at the phone on the wall unable to fathom this magnitude of attention. My mother called to tell me Anderson Cooper had sent her a fruit basket. Overnight, my front doorstep brimmed with flowers and gourmet gift baskets from Manhattan's finest purveyors, each network vying to outdo each other in a bid to be the first to get me to break my silence.

Ken and I joined two other couples for a quiet dinner on the harbor. Looking forward to a relaxing and intimate evening out, we dressed nicely and walked a few blocks over to the restaurant where the owner had set up an elegant, candlelit table for us in the back away from prying eyes. After the insane, stressful few days, it was nice to relax to share some laughs with our friends.

As we lingered over coffee and dessert, a well-dressed man at the bar rose and walked over to our table. He complimented us on what a beautiful table we were and said he was thankful that I had some time to enjoy with my friends at last. He then introduced himself as an *ABC News* executive and handed me his business card. He had been eavesdropping on us the entire evening. I felt invaded and was both angry and frightened. The restaurant owner saw what was happening and escorted the man out quickly. When we left the restaurant a while later, he was waiting on the sidewalk and tried to speak to me once more. The men in our party blocked him from approaching me. I realized then that even in my own neighborhood there would be no privacy.

The next evening, I attended an Alcoholics Anonymous meeting in a church up the street. Midway through the meeting, a friend came over and whispered in my ear that there were several reporters and a cameraman outside the church. I left through a side door and retreated to my home, once again passing through the phalanx of reporters and cameramen.

That evening, Ken's brother Jack came to check on me with a young woman in tow whom he had just begun seeing. She was pleasant and quite likeable and we hit it off well. Ken quickly whipped up an impromptu treat and the four of us spent a lovely evening together. We said good night and Jack and the young woman headed out. Later that night, Jack returned to the house, near tears. As it turned out, the young woman was a reporter who had befriended him in an attempt to get to me. She had come clean once she had gotten her story, "At Home With Steven Slater." Ken and I went to bed, heartbroken for Jack.

No sooner had we turned out the lights than there came a scratching at the bedroom window. I turned on the lights to reveal a man removing the screen from the window just as another shoved a camera against the glass and started snapping pictures of the two of us in our bedroom. This was the final straw. I had heard things about the media, but I never knew they could be this unscrupulous. It had gone from flattering to surreal to positively frightening.

I knew I needed help navigating these uncharted waters so I contacted Howard Bragman of *15 Minutes Public Relations* who had so adeptly guided such luminous clients as Monica Lewinsky through trying moments. We met for a classic power breakfast at the Regency Hotel on Park Avenue where I was introduced to what would become my team of high-powered entertainment lawyers, prominent and high-profile defense attorney Daniel Horowitz, just off the Bernie Madoff trial who would now provide my legal defense, and a poised and highly efficient assistant who would help me juggle all of my new commitments as I prepared to foray into the whirlwind of media and endorsements. This was a true Dream Team if ever assembled. Howard's first move was to make an announcement that all media requests would be channeled through him. Suddenly, the phone stopped ringing and I could breathe once more. I could walk through my neighborhood in peace again.

I would break my silence with back-to-back interviews with *Larry King Live*, *Good Morning America*, the *CBS Early Show*, and the *Today Show*. Larry King would lead the way with the exclusive interview followed by the three morning shows the next day. In order to pull this off, Howard, Dan Horowitz, Kenneth, and I were flown First Class on United to Los Angeles to tape the *Larry King Live* show a few days in advance.

Although I had never had any form of media training other than an hour in Howard's New York apartment, I felt confident and at ease. I was prepared to face difficult questions. I was well aware that my behavior on the airplane was less than stellar and I was ready to face my drinking and my lack of professionalism squarely. I knew that if I owned my truth no one could use it against me. I flew to Los Angeles ready to take it on the chin. "The truth shall set you free" was my motto.

Arriving at the CNN Studios in the chauffeured Escalade, we were quickly ushered onto the studio. The space was compact and efficient and I was surprised at how few people it took to run the operation. I was invited to relax and help myself to refreshments in a comfortable green room. The whole affair was very low-key and surprisingly informal.

I had always seen Larry King as an irascible and caustic figure but when I was led to the soundstage to meet him, I found him to be diminutive and humble, and hospitable from the get-go. He greeted me warmly and asked me a few questions with keen interest. Despite the fact that we were about to have a heart-to-heart in front of over a million viewers, I felt at ease. We took our places opposite one another and quickly rolled into the interview with no rehearsal. It all flowed naturally and easily. I spoke candidly with humor, grace, and a bit of charm. The camera was kind. Larry King made it easy and we fell into an easy, comfortable rapport. I spoke at length about the lack of civility in air travel and feeling undervalued as an employee and I came across as well-informed, relatable, and insightful. The interview ran on the 26th of August, 2010, and was a resounding success, setting the tone for the media appearances ahead.

Running the gauntlet of New York morning news shows on the 27th of August was both exhilarating and taxing. A town car picked me and Ken up early in the morning and drove us into the city and straight to the *CBS Early Show* where I was immediately thrown into the chair for hair and makeup then ushered onto the set where I gave an upbeat, light interview with Maggie Rodriguez that got me warmed up for the day ahead. From there, it was back into the car and crosstown to NBC for the *Today Show*.

The *Today Show* was a study in controlled chaos with technicians and assistants bustling in and out of the brightly lit studio. I was to be interviewed by Matt Lauer, who sat tall and lanky in a chair eating a salad out of a Tupperware container. We exchanged a friendly greeting and took our places on set amongst the flurry of activity whirling about. In short order, we began the interview which seemed friendly enough, at first. He asked roughly the same interview questions I had just fielded at CBS and I told my story once more. Suddenly, he ambushed. "So, you're HIV positive and an alcoholic?" My blood boiled. Knowing this was live television with over a million people watching, I knew I had to remain classy and could not afford a sharp retort to his low blow.

"Recovering alcoholic, Matt."

"One day at a time?" he replied. I simply gave my sweetest flight attendant smile and the interview continued on. From my previous experiences over the past week with the media, I had known to be prepared for anything and I was pleased with my response. But I was reminded of the lengths to which an unscrupulous reporter would go for a splashy story. I believe Lauer's tacky query only served to make me look more sympathetic but it was certainly a lowlight of my media experience.

After the interview, I was whisked away with a full face of makeup to ABC for my third and favorite interview, *Good Morning America*, with Elizabeth Vargas. By now I was in rare form and in the full swing of things and gave a fantastic and funny interview that had the studio in stitches. I loved working with Elizabeth Vargas and would be her guest twice more in the year to come on *20/20* and an ABC special. She was elegant, ironic, and would become by far my favorite media professional. By the time I returned to my home in Belle Harbor, I was exhausted but feeling very accomplished.

I had become something of a media sensation. At once, offers and opportunities began pouring in. I was offered a number of endorsement deals hawking everything from energy drinks to weight loss products. Some of the offers were quite lucrative, including a gig as the national spokesperson for an upstart telecommunications company which I enjoyed wholeheartedly. But because I was embroiled in an ongoing criminal case, I had to pass on most everything, especially anything that would send the wrong message to the courts. Within days, I was booked on countless television shows in New York and Los Angeles from *Regis and Kelly* to *Ricki Lake*, and *Geraldo Rivera*. I was crossing the country once a week to make an appearance and my face was in print at least weekly. I was named to the Out 100 as one of the one hundred most influential LGBT people of the year and feted at the OUT gala in New York.

A highlight of my celebrity experience was appearing in a four-page spread in *New York Magazine* entitled "Steven Slater's Landing" in which Michael Idov chronicled a day in the life of Steven Slater. I felt like a Hollywood starlet arriving at Siren Studios on Hollywood Boulevard for the photoshoot. Jaunita Lyons of Redken did my hair and makeup and made me feel like Cinderella. I was shot by renowned photographer Jeff Minton of *Sports Illustrated Swimsuit Edition* fame who led me through turns and dips to Michael Jackson's "It's the Falling in Love" until we got the perfect shot of my face brimming with impish mischievousness which appeared as a full page in the magazine.

From Hollywood, we caravanned over Laurel Canyon to the Burbank Airport where we set up shop at the end of the runway and took a number of candid shots of me chasing airplanes in my uniform. The temperature was 105 degrees that afternoon and the shots required an assistant to run into Vineland Avenue and stop traffic for me to run ahead of a technician bearing a giant light, then Jeff ran along behind us with his camera while I played my wacky role. We did this a dozen times but in the end the magazine ran a cheeky film strip of a safety demonstration I improvised in the studio. The final shots were both brilliant and glamorous and it was such an honor to work with Jeff.

The team and I had several meetings in Los Angeles with television producers to discuss reality television opportunities which always seemed to have the same premise: helping people quit their jobs in over-the-top and spectacular ways. I was always half-hearted about these discussions as they always seemed salacious and in poor taste. I was, however, down to do something in which we helped people find their true, authentic calling and liberate themselves from the enslavement of an unsatisfying career path, but no one seemed to want to make an investment in the actual participants but rather, only wanted to do things like skydive out of an office building and call it a day.

Of much interest were two meetings with major New York publishing houses to discuss a memoir. Riding the elevator in the Conde Nast building was something akin to a moment of arrival and a dream come true. I have always treasured the written word and the rarefied environment of the storied publishing house was exhilarating. I would love to have pursued the opportunity further, however, I didn't have anything terribly profound to say at that moment in my life, and that was evident.

A great deal of my ambivalence towards cashing in on my newfound fame had to do with my own inner conflict with how that fame had come to be in the first place. What occurred on the airplane was an alcoholic relapse followed by a manic episode. While much of society and most of the media was touting me as America's new folk hero, in my own mind this whole affair was a source of great shame. I saw nothing heroic or noble about the circumstances that had brought me this attention and while it was heady and intoxicating being the object of such adoration and attention, deep in my heart, I felt fraudulent and unworthy. The more attention and validation I received, the worse I felt. To me, it all felt like a house of cards. I had been honest, I admitted that I was drinking on the airplane and that I had been remiss in managing my mental health leading to the meltdown. But even to me, much of the circumstances surrounding that flight remained hazy, nebulous at best. I could not in good conscience accept the adulation of a fawning public for an event that I felt was scandalous at best.

To make matters worse, now that this thing had taken on a life of its own, I could not share this secret with anyone. This led me to feel extraordinarily lonely in the midst of this swirling adulation. Instead, I retreated deeper into my secret and my shame.

And now, I was expected to perform, to play the part of America's new folk hero, full of bravado and sass. Suddenly, I was a brand and a product. A product I had to sell, a product that I did not believe in for one moment. A shoddy product I just could not get behind. To make matters worse, I now had investors in its success. It was a tall order I just wasn't up to.

CHAPTER 12

I n addition to the stress of my newfound celebrity, my mother's
health continued to decline. I felt more and more conflict being
away from California. It soon became apparent that time was
running out and I was needed at home. I began to curtail my
New York trips as much as possible.

Dan Horowitz worked out a plea deal in which I was able to live
full-time in California and appear in court in New York once a month
for a progress report. As part of the plea deal, I was ordered into
mental health counseling and visits with a Manhattan psychiatrist. I
began making the monthly commute, staying with Ken in our Belle
Harbor house for one or two nights a month before hurrying back to
California as quickly as possible. A high school friend, Robin, and her
husband Aaron graciously agreed to stay with my mother and took
excellent care of her while I made my New York trips. I was very
grateful   for   their   assistance.

Toward the end of 2011, my mother's health declined rapidly
and it was readily apparent that the end was near. I had an upcoming
mandatory court appearance and one remaining fine to pay which made
the trip necessary. Missing the court appearance would result in a jail
sentence. With much reluctance, I agreed to take the trip, checking in
with Robin and Aaron from New York throughout the day. While
away, my mother took a turn for the worse. Ken and I rushed to
Kennedy Airport for our flight back to California but while changing

planes in Phoenix, we learned that my mother passed away while we were in flight. There had been earlier, nonstop flights we could have selected had we any idea she would not have made it through the day. The guilt and shame I carried over missing her death haunted me for several years and led to much self-harm.

A year sober, I finished my probation in New York. Out from under the threat of jail time, I was free to live my life as I desired once more. I inherited the house, which was paid off, and a sizable inheritance. I began to remodel and undertook an elaborate landscaping project I did mostly myself, planting a variety of Mediterranean and indigenous Western flowers and shrubs. I continued to do my various media appearances and went to work on a few writing projects for magazines and websites.

I continued to attend Alcoholics Anonymous meetings where I made some new friends, a couple of whom were in between places to stay. Living alone in a four-bedroom house left me feeling very lonely so I invited three young men I met in AA to stay with me. It wasn't long before we all relapsed together and I had turned my beautiful home into a hotbed of sex, drugs, and rock and roll. I discovered that crystal meth was half price in California and my young friends all had numerous connections to the best product in Southern California. Soon we had tricks coming and going at all hours of the day and night, and drugs flowed like water.

Ken had grown resentful of all the media attention so I mostly curtailed my trips back to New York, much preferring the company of my young accomplices to that of my sober partner. I put myself on the dating apps and hookup sites and was soon traveling all over the greater Los Angeles area in search of drug-fueled sex. It was a blast and I was having the time of my life with no one looking over my shoulder for the first time in ages. It was all enormous fun and I was like a kid in a candy store.

But once more, I had forgotten about the lethal combination of bipolar disorder and methamphetamine. Initially, the combination brought joyful results. My hallucinations tended towards the sounds of acclaim and applause when I walked into rooms or I heard impish laughter from the corners of my room. I stopped sleeping and stayed up for days and nights on end, which was highly useful in my pursuit of endless drugs and sex.

By now, my trips to New York had become infrequent at best. Ken and I argued incessantly and he preferred the company of his local friends to spending time with me. I had all but stopped returning entirely after he had left me sitting at JFK long after midnight insisting I take a cab to the house, unwilling to travel seven miles to collect me from the airport after I had just flown 2,500 miles through the night to be with him. This had pretty much told me everything I needed to know about the status of our relationship, and I stayed more or less West Coast-based since.

I scheduled a trip for mid-October in 2012 more out of a sense of obligation than anything else, yet as the departure date grew closer, I found myself unable to pull it together, caught up in a cycle of heavy partying with my new California friends and roommates. When it became apparent that I wouldn't make my flight, I blew the trip off and texted Ken. He was furious. It had not been the first time in recent months that I had either no-showed or begged off at the last moment.

Caught up in the all-consuming intoxication of yet another drug-fueled orgy, I paid little attention to the news of an intense storm gathering strength and speed off the Atlantic coast. When the sun rose on the morning of October 29th, I had been up for days, strung out and sleep-deprived, entertaining three men who had been going strong with me for the last 48 hours. I was jarred back to reality by a video clip that Ken texted me of pounding storm surge ripping away the deck of our beautiful beachfront house. I was confused. The hurricane was projected to pass far out to sea, never to make landfall. I was far too blasted to process this or to be of any assistance, so I simply set the phone back on the nightstand and continued the party.

A short while later, a concerned Belle Harbor neighbor called, informing me that everyone on the block had evacuated but that Ken was refusing to leave our home. I called him at once. I could hear the virulent storm in the background. Ken was in shock. He sounded upbeat and chipper, as if in the midst of a grand adventure and insisting that there was nothing he couldn't handle there. After all, he reminded me, he had been a lifeguard and was a certified physical trainer. He would wait a little while longer and see what more the storm brought in. He then grew sharp and asked if I was high. We had a loud argument and then he hung up on me. *Fine*, I thought, *if that's how he wants to play this, fuck him*. I turned off my phone and slid back into bed with my waiting suitors, shrugging aside the imminent danger bearing down upon New York.

Turning my phone back on 24 hours later, after seeing my guests out exhausted and spent, there were dozens of messages from concerned friends and neighbors. The news was grim. My home was leveled and Ken was missing. My seaside retreat was destroyed. The restful seafoam green and aquamarine living room chock-a-block with nautical treasures and artful black and white photography was no more. The romantic, candle-strewn, wicker bedroom so cozy and snug where the din of the rolling waves lulled us to sleep each night was now on the seafloor.

My heart lurched. Now sober and growing more so by the moment, I ran to the television and viewed the sickening images of what had once been our idyllic beachside community, now in ruins. There was, of course, no phone service and communication with Belle Harbor had been rendered impossible. I spent the horrifying next 24 hours devoid of information fearing the worst, transfixed before the television. It was more than I could bear. I called my connect in Oxnard, bought myself a sack of dope, and invited some friends over. I waited respectfully until the news came in that Ken was safe with friends in Brooklyn. Then I got high as hell and never looked back.

I found him on Craigslist Personals. We had emailed back and forth over the course of a couple of prior New York trips and now we were meeting at last. We shared a taste for crack cocaine. When I arrived at his well-worn, tenement apartment, I was instantly intrigued by his goatee, shaved head, and stocky build. He greeted me shirtless in jeans and bare feet. In a gravelly Brooklyn accent, he invited me directly into the bedroom where a crack pipe and ample supply of rock lay waiting. I had scored doubly with this one.

He lay back on the bed, his legs outstretched and crossed at the ankle, and motioned me to sit beside him. He picked up the glass pipe and took a good, deep hit. He passed it to me and I did the same, my head swirling and heart racing. This was good shit. Greedily, I lit the pipe and pulled deeply again. He smiled appreciatively then took the pipe back and took another long hit for himself.

"Get naked," he commanded, leering appreciatively at me, and nodded to the floor beside the bed. I quickly obliged and lost my clothes, standing naked for his appraisal. "Nice. Fuckin whore," he purred, lifting the glass pipe again and squinting over it as he regarded me while lighting it once more. He patted the bed next to him and I quickly sat down beside him again. He held the pipe up to my mouth, lit it, and fed me another hit. This was hot as hell. Then he set the pipe back down on the table and turned to watch me as I exhaled.

Suddenly with no warning, he punched me hard in the face. Blood, hot and metallic, spurted from my nose and poured into my mouth and back down my throat, causing me to choke as I lost my balance and fell backwards, startled and shocked. No sooner had I floundered onto my back then he was grabbing my head and lurching me back forward, forcing my face against the jagged metal zipper of his jeans and holding me tightly there. "FUCKING FAGGOT! YOU WANNA DIE TODAY?" he yelled as he threw me to the floor where I landed with a resounding thud and cowered into a fetal position. At once, he was over me, stomping my head as I cowered, my hands over my ears. "STUPID. FUCKING. CRACK. WHORE!" He was screaming with rage, each enunciated word eliciting another blow as he stomped powerfully down upon my neck from above.

After a hard kick square in the face, he grabbed me from under the arms and flung me like a rag doll back onto the bed, face down. He was an animal, savage, superhuman, fueled by cocaine and hate. I knew in that moment that only by surrendering could I hope to survive. I felt his powerful fingers wrap around my neck from behind as he lifted my torso up off the bed and suddenly I saw the tiny plastic wastebasket beside the bed into which my head was about to be stuffed. With unrelenting strength, he propelled my face down into the can and my lips and nose were forced back open against the unyielding plastic, forming a perfect seal and cutting off oxygen as my body froze in a 45 degree angle, my hips and pelvis jutting up onto the mattress. Unable to breathe, I began to panic. I tried to scream but my lungs were frozen in place. Abject terror washed over me as I was consumed by a fear like I had never known.

His brutal, rough hands forced my legs wide and I felt a pain beyond that which I had ever experienced. I felt a searing heat and an excruciating tear as he rammed into me and I knew it would be the last thing I felt before leaving Earth. A crushing sorrow descended upon me as I realized this would be how I would be remembered by my loved ones. I felt hot tears of shame in my eyes as I began to black out, my chest now beginning to spasm in suffocation and my body twitching and shaking as life slipped out of me. Everything began to fade to black in perfect, insular silence.

Suddenly, I was tumbling now, spinning, turning, dizzy, then blinded in the bright living room as he stood above me, straddling me, the wastebasket held in his hands above his head. A hard kick to the ribs brought my attention home and I doubled over in pain and fear once more. "Fucking faggot drug addict," he hissed and spat down into my face, then turned and sat back on the bed and hit the pipe once more.

A moment later, I felt a blinding flash of pain as he kicked me hard in the anus. I howled and covered myself with my hands then suddenly I felt a chunk of hair ripped from my head. He was pulling me now by my hair as I clawed at the chipped linoleum in the entryway trying to push myself along with him, my legs flailing. He dropped me roughly, facing a full-length mirror.

"LOOK AT YOURSELF YOU PATHETIC FAGGOT!" he screamed, and slapped me hard across my bloodied face. "THIS IS

THIS WHAT YOU WANTED, FAGGOT! ISN'T IT? ISN'T IT?" he demanded, now inches from my face as I began to sob.

He kept me there in front of the mirror for much of the afternoon, punishing me and making me look at myself. He punished me for contacting him on the Internet and for stupidly coming to a stranger's apartment. He punished me for using drugs and for my addiction. He punished me for wanting him. And when he was done with me, he threw my clothes into the hall and locked the door behind me. I dressed on the stairs and staggered catatonic into a corner bodega a few blocks away where the young Middle Eastern owner pieced me back together with tears in his eyes. I hid in my hotel room until a few days later, when I left New York and never returned.

To avoid calling attention to my increasing drug use and the mounting traffic in and out of my home, I began staying in seedy motels around Los Angeles. One night, I invited a man to my room off the Internet. Scott was rugged and rough around the edges with an easy, cocky virility. He was straight, although we did fool around a little. Scott was something of a drifter who worked his way across the city by preying on lonely, middle-aged, gay men who fell for his hard-luck story and his manipulative and seductive physicality.

It wasn't long before Scott's mercurial moodiness and penchant for violent outbursts became evident and I never knew what mood he would be in when I picked him up for the evening. He was also a drug dealer and I quickly became one of his top customers. In no time, I was helping him make deliveries in my Mini Cooper. One night, Scott sent me to the Valley alone to make a delivery to a customer, Aaron, a mild-mannered and amiable businessman, on his birthday. Scott also instructed me to sleep with Aaron and to show him a good time for his 40th. Aaron and I got high and had a great time together that night. In the course of the evening, Aaron confided to me that Scott had been trying to force his way into staying in his apartment and using it for a base for his operation. Scott had recently threatened Aaron's life. Scott had been taking money from Aaron by force and he was frightened for his safety. Aaron implored me to get away from Scott while I still could and told me that anyone who got involved with Scott eventually met with harm.

Within a few weeks, Scott got involved with a lovely young woman in Beverly Hills and moved in with her. They were the picture of domestic bliss and Scott was ever the doting boyfriend. She knew nothing of the drug dealing, which continued surreptitiously, and Scott started work as the handyman on the building on Roxbury Drive. Within a few months, the woman had gone missing from the scene, and suddenly the apartment was cleared out. Shortly thereafter, Aaron's furniture and personal belongings started to appear in the apartment one by one and there was no mention of the young woman again.

One late night in the apartment when Scott and I were extremely high, I brought it up. Scott flew into a rage screaming that there had never been a woman and that I was a fucking drug addict who had lost my mind, that it had been his apartment and his alone all along. Emboldened by the crystal meth coursing through my veins, I asked him how it came to be that Aaron's furniture was now in the apartment. Shaking with rage, Scott snatched up my keys off the table and grabbed me roughly. He pulled me out the door and down the stairs and towards my car parked at the curb. He shoved me into the passenger seat, slammed the door, then got into the car and started it. He leaned in close to my face and glowered into my eyes. "Aaron died alone and afraid," he seethed.

Then he started the car and pulled out into traffic. Scott was insane, out of his mind as he careened down the late night city streets at high speed as I sat terrified, paralyzed in the passenger seat. He was racing now, swerving through intersections and cutting off traffic as I prayed he wouldn't kill us both with his drug-fueled recklessness. He seemed lost in thought, in deep consideration. I didn't dare speak nor even move for fear of setting him off further. He raced across the city for hours. I was terrified, not knowing our destination nor what fate awaited me upon arrival.

Then at once, he seemed to reconsider and turned the car back towards the apartment. He pulled up in front of the building and ordered me back inside. I followed him timidly up the stairs, and he led me back inside, closing the door behind me.

Back in the darkened apartment, he was quiet, deliberate. He crossed the floor and picked up a meth pipe off of the table then pulled a kitchen chair out from the table and set it in the middle of the room. At once, he dropped his jeans down around his ankles and sat down in the chair. He motioned me over and pointed to the floor. He held a torch to the pipe and took a long pull and exhaled the white, thick smoke. Hate burned in his eyes. "The way I like it," he hissed.

Obediently, I got on my knees and took his hard cock in my fist, trying to steady myself from shaking. I could not meet his rage-filled eyes. He blew a cloud of billowy smoke in my face, and I went down on him hesitantly. I had just begun to service him when he cocked his fist back up high as if to strike a blow against my face. I flinched and cowered as his clenched fist flew forward then stopped just a half inch from my face as I tensed for the blow. Instead, he opened his hand and gently and lovingly caressed the back of my head. Confused and bewildered, I paused. Afraid of drawing further ire, I went back to the task at hand. A minute went by then he suddenly raised his fist as if to strike another blow, then once again instead of striking a blow, he caressed my face gently. He was getting off on my terror and confusion. Tears stung my eyes as I began to shake violently. I felt his hands cup my face as he lifted my face toward his. His hate-filled eyes met and held mine. "Alone and afraid," he whispered. "Alone and afraid."

Then he pushed me backward onto the floor, stood up, and pulled up his pants. He took my keys and walked out leaving me crumpled, alone, sobbing on the apartment floor.

Now once more addicted to crystal meth, I returned a few days later for my fix. Scott was pleasant, controlled. I breathed a sigh of relief. We got high together. He told me he needed me to make a run for him. This was odd, as I usually drove for him while he ran in and made his drops. He handed me an envelope with an insane quantity of meth inside. Then he handed me a scale. I was high as hell but I wasn't stupid. In California, getting busted with drugs and a scale together equaled automatic distribution charges. He was setting me up. I was shocked but I played along, and zipped up the items in my backpack. He wrote down an address in Santa Monica on a piece of paper and handed it to me. On the one hand, I was horrified. But on the other hand, I was grateful that it had come to this and not physical harm. This I could outsmart.

I got into my car and pulled away, my mind racing at a thousand miles per hour. Presumably, he had tipped off the cops. Would I get busted en route or would it happen at the destination? I drove a few blocks, scanning the rearview mirror and expecting to be pulled over at any second, my heart in my throat. I drove a few miles down Venice Boulevard then pulled into an alley and parked the car. I figured it would be better to get busted on foot than behind the wheel. I threw my backpack over my shoulder and started walking. A block away, I spotted a Chinese restaurant and walked inside and directly into the men's room. I opened my bag, lifted the trash bag out of the trashcan, and hid the lot in the bottom of the can. Then I replaced the liner. I walked out of the restaurant and back to my car, then drove directly to the Beverly Hills Police Department and pulled up in front of the station house.

I walked inside terrified and shaking, and up to the duty officer at the window. I was still high as hell; I could barely formulate the words to explain what had happened. I spilled my long and rambling tale about the missing woman, about Jeff confiding to me about Scott's threats, and about what Scott had told me about Jeff having died afraid and alone. I gave the officer the address of the Roxbury Drive apartment and told them of the endless cache of drugs to be found there. I explained that all of this could be validated by the stash in the trashcan of the Chinese restaurant on Venice Boulevard. The duty officer cocked his head and looked at me incredulously and asked me if everything I told him was indeed true. I swore it was so and he said he would send an officer to the restaurant to investigate. I then realized I was standing in a police station blasted on crystal meth and had probably best get the hell out of there stat, so I turned on my heel and bid a hasty retreat to my car and pulled away onto Beverly Boulevard, fresh out of options, unsure of my next move.

CHAPTER 13

The officer hadn't believed me. Of that, I was certain. High as hell, I had made little sense. And yet, I had tipped the LAPD to Scott's operation. They would be obligated to pay a visit. Scott would know it had been me, that much was sure. And what if I was wrong about the whole affair? What if this had been a routine delivery after all? Just suppose, I had just done him dirty, not made the drop, and disappeared with the goods? Scott had been to my house and he knew my car. There was nowhere to run. I was a dead man, however this played out.

The more I drove through Beverly Hills, the more frightened I became. I was in a highly agitated state, amped up on meth and in panic. I drove the Westside in circles in an increasing frenzy of terror as I considered my dilemma. I began to flip into a manic episode, losing touch with reality. Suddenly, ghostly figures stood staring from the street corners, whispering ominous warnings and pointing toward imaginary pursuers. "That way," they motioned, directing me toward safety as I drove on into the twilight of the setting sun. Racing down Beverly Boulevard, five attractive men in suits stood atop the roof of the Chase Bank at the corner of Fairfax pointing east, directing me to safety. All of Los Angeles seemed to be conspiring for my safety as I drove through the night.

Still, I knew Scott was closing in on me. Soon, he would spot me, seeking revenge. My hunter green Mini on the L.A. streets would be a sure give away. I had to ditch the car, fast. I pulled over on a residential side street in the Mid-Wilshire District, grabbed my backpack, and fled on foot, voices screaming in my head, *Run!* In my intoxication and panic, I quickly became disoriented and soon found myself lost and unsure which way to go. I hoped to find Santa Monica Boulevard in West Hollywood and the shelter of the Ramada Hotel but nothing appeared familiar and soon I realized I was passing the same apartment buildings and restaurants time and again. Terrified and overwhelmed, I began to hyperventilate and cry. Passersby began to creep closer, their eyes hollow and vacant. "He's near," a woman whispered. Another pushed a baby carriage past and hissed, "Your soul in the carriage." I screamed and ran out into La Cienega Boulevard as traffic screeched to a stop and crowds cheered my near demise. Hot tears stung my eyes as I wandered for hours, often cowering in doorways and shrubbery as people and cars passed by on the streets. I was certain Scott was close at hand.

Suddenly, I saw the CNN tower blazing above like a beacon of hope. Someone there would remember me. They would help me. Certainly they would not let me die on the street hunted like prey. I started off in a run toward the brightly lit tower but it soon disappeared between the tall buildings of Hollywood. In despair, I cried out, lost. I circled for hours, catching occasional glimpses of the tower but could not find my way to it.

I heard his boots on the pavement behind me, felt his heavy breath in my ear. It would be soon. He would be merciless. "Alone and afraid," hissed passersby as I stumbled past, blinded by tears and gasping for breath. My eyes fell on a convenience store ahead. I would do it before he could. I would be merciful in the task. Left to him, I would suffer unspeakable brutality.

I walked in, resigned and surprisingly collected, and surveyed the options. I selected a gallon of antifreeze, a container of charcoal fluid, and a Bic lighter. I paid the disinterested Indian store clerk, and stepped out into the still night air. Walking on, I chuckled to myself at the irony as I passed a fire station, then turned onto Vine Street and headed north toward the legendary corner of Hollywood and Vine, awash in garish neon.

Suddenly, he was upon me. I screamed, but joyful people walked past in twos and threes laughing and joking with one another enjoying a warm, California night, unaware of the horrors befalling me. No one heard my screams, nor saw the madman as he wrapped his thick fingers around my neck. And then, he was gone.

I had to act fast before he could return to finish his task. I quickly unscrewed the top to the antifreeze and hoisted it to my lips. It was heavy and slippery on my tongue as I guzzled it hungrily. I guzzled down as much as I could until my stomach felt full. Then I threw the container, 3/4 full, to the sidewalk. The rainbow-hued fluid splashed onto the sidewalk around me. I flung my backpack off my shoulders and onto the sidewalk as well. It contained my laptop which held many secrets, the least of which was emails between Scott and I. I had to destroy this evidence at once. I removed the top from the charcoal lighter and sprayed a healthy squirt onto the backpack and across my shoes and was about to turn it to my body when I suddenly began to retch violently. I dropped the bottle to the ground and doubled over in pain. A stream of foamy vomit flew forth from my mouth and down my front.

I knew I had better act fast if I was going to set this fire. I quickly flicked the Bic and touched it to my backpack, setting a bright blaze that lit the facade of 1600 Vine Street in an eerie, orange glow. I doubled over, falling to the sidewalk, between the stars of Charlton Heston and Arleen Dahl, feeling the warmth of the flames against my face as I started to black out. Suddenly, I could no longer see. There was a perfect stillness and I felt a peace like never before.

Then at once, the voice of an African-American man, urgent and frightened, was in my ear.

"Oh MAN, what did you DO?" he asked, breaking the reverie.

"I drank antifreeze," I choked out, meekly.

"Hold on, man, just HOLD ON!" he implored. At once, he was banging on the glass door of 1600 Vine. I heard the sound of a metal key turning in the lock and the door swung open. "You gotta help us, man!" he called out. "This man drank some antifreeze!" he yelled, urgently.

"I'll call 911!" replied a man excitedly from within the building. I heard hurried footsteps from within as the man inside rushed away to call. Then my angel was back, crouched at my side, his hand on my shoulder. "Just HOLD ON MAN, they're on the way. I'll stay with you as long as I can. I GOT you man, Just stay with me, STAY WITH ME, YOU HEAR ME?" His voice trembled and his hands shook and I grasped his arm and held on tight in my blindness. Soon, I heard the distant wail of a lonely siren in the night growing louder, approaching. "HERE THEY COME, THAT'S FOR YOU, MAN!" my angel assured me in his shaking voice as I coughed and sputtered. "YOU GOTTA HANG ON!" he begged.

"I'll stay as long as I can," he reassured, tearfully now. And I believed him. And soon the siren stopped and I was being lifted up and into an ambulance but all I heard was his frightened voice clear in my ear as he was saying, "I'm here, man, I'm here."

And I held on, for him. I never saw his face but I will never forget his voice so true and kind. They call Los Angeles the "City of Angels." And that night, I learned exactly why.

The room was blindingly bright when I came to in the emergency room at Kaiser Permanente on Sunset, unable to move. I struggled against the heavy, brown leather restraints that anchored me to the bed. I remembered nothing of the events on the street in Hollywood, knowing only that I was pursued by a sardonic madman. I tried to rise again only to be snapped back firmly by the restraints once more. I screamed as all-consuming panic rose from the depths of my psyche. I twisted against the wrist straps which only caused them to cut into my skin, ratcheting my panic to further heights of insanity. I screamed out, alternating for help and to be let go. Two nurses arrived at my bedside and tried to explain to me that I was in the emergency room, and urging me to relax.

Within moments, a cocky, young physician appeared at the foot of my bed, a sideways sneer across his face. Out of my mind, reliving childhood trauma from the years of brutal medical procedures that took place under similar restraint, I kicked and clawed against the leather straps as more nurses and orderlies began pushing my body back against the bed. I flew completely out of my mind with rage, hurling invectives at the doctor who stood with his arms crossed, a bemused expression across his face watching me struggle. I believed the physician to be working in concert with Scott, holding me captive until he could arrive to end my life in the most brutal fashion imaginable. I was not going down without a fight. "LET ME UP, MOTHERFUCKER!" I screamed, shaking violently. "I'LL KILL YOU, YOU FUCKING FAGGOT!" I screamed, white-hot, searing pain shooting down my back as I torqued against the restraints. With a dismissive flip of the wrist, the snotty young doctor decreed I be transferred to a psychiatric hospital for an involuntary 72-hour hold, then turned his back and trotted out of the room. I was now blinded by rage, and emitting sounds that weren't human at the top of my lungs. Suddenly, a syringe plunged deep into my arm and all went black at once.

I awoke in a wood-framed twin bed, beneath a pink blanket marked "County of Los Angeles." I gazed around the room at four snoring men in various stages of undress. Gone was the terror and panic of the night before and I felt rested and restored. I stepped from the bed and into the hallway and glanced toward a bustling nurses' station at the end of the long, brightly lit corridor.

I crept up to the desk and immediately blushed as my eyes fell upon the strapping and disarmingly handsome Latino hunk in a burgundy polo shirt seated at the desk. "Hey there! You must be Steven," he said, his megawatt smile lighting up his chiseled face. "You're just in time for Community Meeting in the group room!" he exclaimed enthusiastically. I had no idea what "Community Meeting" was nor where the "group room" lay, but I would have followed this exquisite Mexican stud with the dazzling white teeth into the fires of hell. I stood there salivating expectantly as he rose and sauntered around the edge of the desk. "This way, Sir," he purred, winking and gesturing to a non-descript patient lounge across the hall where a motley crew of disheveled inmates sat assembled haphazardly around the room, staring at the floor and muttering incoherently to themselves. I was immediately taken aback by the lassitude and malaise of the highly dejected group.

The Spanish stud walked over to a whiteboard at the front of the room. He picked up a pen and began to write the date in block letters. The muscles in his thick and brawny, brown forearms flexed as he nimbly handled the marker. The room spun.

"All right everybody! Do we all know what day it is? Today is February 12th, 2011! It's Wednesday!" he exclaimed resoundingly to no response whatsoever from the medicated audience. "I'm Rene," he continued. Then he turned to the group and smiled proudly. No one stirred. I applauded. "Okay," Rene continued. "Now we will go around the room and say our name and a feeling." He pointed at me. "Steven, would you like to start?" he asked.

"Oh, yes!" I gushed. "May I?" I beamed. "Well, I'm Steven. Hi!" I said, waving briskly to everyone in the room. "And I would say I am… confused!" I threw my head back, gave my best sorority sister laugh, and cocked my head pertly looking into Rene's deep, dreamy, brown eyes. "I mean, um…well, where exactly ARE we, really?"

Renee chuckled good-naturedly, playing along, and responded, "They call this 'Behavioral Health Center, Alhambra.' But trust me, you won't be here long," he said conspiratorially with a smile, scanning the room of barely functioning mouth breathers. Then he moved on trying to draw a feeling out of the next flatlined patient.

It was my late mother's birthday, and I was due on set to start shooting a film that morning. This was not how I had planned this day to go.

At Alhambra, I met a brilliant therapist named Renata who helped me see how the effect of "co-occurring disorder," the simultaneous existence of both a mental health and substance abuse diagnosis, was impacting my life. I saw for the first time in a very real way how I was self-medicating with substances to seek relief from my pre-existing mental illness symptoms. Although I had been to rehab, the emphasis was always on the substance abuse solely. Here, for the first time, I was urged to do a deep dive into my mental illness as well.

Chastened and much wiser for the experience of my psychiatric hospitalization, I returned to my home in Thousand Oaks recommitted to my recovery. I even attended a few Alcoholics Anonymous meetings. But willpower is no match for a powerful addiction run rampant and within a few weeks, I was back in the motels downtown.

Having crossed the line into IV drug abuse, the crystal meth now had a much more profound effect on my brain and psychiatric condition than ever before. One particularly hardcore run of partying left me wandering Beverly Hills manic and disoriented for two nights in a state of paranoia and panic after walking out of my motel room on San Vicente Boulevard shirtless and without shoes, unable to find my way back to the motel. I relived my ghastly "soul-in-the-baby-carriage" fantasy and ran screaming down Melrose from every baby stroller that passed, believing every infant was a tiny grim reaper come to steal my life.

Forty-eight hours into hallucination and hysteria, I began pounding on the bay windows of a house screaming for help until I finally laid down in a driveway, exhausted, and sobbed for hours. Out of the corner of my eye, I noticed an ambulance pass by and then a while later, I noticed another. By the time three ambulances had passed, some flicker of self-preservation deep within had kicked in and I rose and started walking heavily and exhausted in the direction they traveled. I stumbled and sobbed, shirtless and shoeless past the tony boutiques and trendy eateries of Robertson Boulevard as passersby swerved and parted to let me through. Suddenly, like a shimmering desert mirage, the word "EMERGENCY" hovered before my bleary eyes. I had arrived at Cedars-Sinai Medical Center. I let out a wail and stumbled through the sliding doors, then fell flat onto the floor, screaming in hysterics, once again believing I was about to be murdered by some unseen pursuer.

A security guard helped me up and to the admitting window where I was told to take a seat in a crowded waiting room in which there were no seats available. I curled up in a fetal position in a corner on the cold tile floor and continued to sob as onlookers looked away awkwardly. Suddenly, an elegant, well-dressed Persian woman jumped up from her seat and started screaming across the room. "Help this man! This is not an animal! Can you not see his pain? Do something!" The woman was suddenly at the desk demanding a pillow and blanket and in a moment, she was at my side on the floor propping my head up gently and covering me with the blanket, stroking my hair as I cried. I was so grateful for her humanity and kindness and I was reminded of the gentleman in Hollywood who stayed with me on the street until help arrived. Shortly, my name was called and the woman helped me to my feet and guided me by the arm to the door, handing me off to a nurse who sat me on a stretcher.

I was parked and abandoned in a hallway where I experienced a terrifying psychotic episode. Each person who passed, real or imagined, turned their head and cursed me. I believed I had struck a young girl with my car and that an ambulance had brought us both to the hospital. Now, no one would tell me the girl's fate. People stood nearby in small clusters discussing the accident and shaking their heads. I kept calling out, screaming and begging for news of the child but no one would tell me if the child had survived. As the night went on, it became clear that she had died. I kept begging for forgiveness but no one would speak to me. Later, I hallucinated that everyone who passed by spat in my face. As the night progressed, I began to overhear plans for my execution. I begged and pleaded for my life, but I was only taunted by all who passed in the hallway.

And suddenly in my grief, someone brought me a shirt and a pair of yellow scruffy hospital socks and I was released into a pouring rain storm. The sky was gray and the streets deserted and I believed that I had been so evil in killing the young girl that the entire city had abandoned me and left me behind to die alone. I wandered up a deserted Robertson Boulevard looking in the windows of the empty boutiques. I cried for my long-lost parents and my son and the beautiful life I had once known. And then I found a quiet place on the grounds of the Pacific Design Center and lay down to die.

I must have fallen asleep for a short time. When I woke up, traffic whizzed by on the Boulevard and people passed on the sidewalks. I was soaked and shivering when I wandered into a Coffee Bean & Tea Leaf in my soaking wet socks. I took my place in line and the woman in front of me turned around and looked down at my wet feet, gave me a warm, sweet smile, and told me to go ahead. I got a coffee and muffin and sat at a table and listened to the discordant din of cacophonous voices in my head offering conflicting advice on my next move. The better part of that afternoon was spent wandering down Wilshire in seek of shelter while arguing with angry, internal voices. I took a hotel room in Koreatown and spent the night in terror, hiding from the sound of an angry, armed mob gathered just outside my door. In the morning, I called a friend who picked me up and drove me directly to Los Robles Hospital in Thousand Oaks for another overnight stay. I was utterly exhausted and clearly beyond my ability to function.

My best thinking after the Cedars-Sinai debacle convinced me that Los Angeles must be the problem. I sourced a new supplier 80 miles north in sleepy Oxnard, in the heart of the Ventura County agricultural district where no one knew me and where, to my knowledge, no one wanted me dead, yet. In Oxnard, the supply came straight from Mexico, pure and unadulterated. It was also half price, allowing me to double up on my quantities. What could go wrong?

I began hunkering down at a rundown bungalow motel off Pacific Coast Highway, just outside of town. With mirrored ceilings and in-room Jacuzzis, the Parakeet Lodge was a cliché no-tell motel. One sultry summer night, I poured myself an Inglenook, filled the jacuzzi with scalding water, and fired up the jets. Then I eased into the swirling broil and shot myself with an enormous issue that had me seeing stars in seconds.

By now, I had long passed the point where I could shoot meth without instantly crossing into psychosis. Suddenly I heard the heavy boots of a SWAT team assembling on the roof about to repel through the motel room windows.

I lunged forth from the steaming waters and into my clothes, jumped into my car, and pulled out onto the highway just narrowly averting the imminent raid. I congratulated myself on giving the cops the slip. But my heart sank when I realized I had left the drugs and paraphernalia scattered around the room. This of course presented a huge problem. I had to run and I had to run fast. I accelerated through 80, then 90 miles per hour onto the Pacific Coast Highway and headed south towards Los Angeles.

Suddenly, the Mini Cooper lifted gently off the surface of the highway and began to hover airborne, suspended about 50 feet above the roadway as in the distance approached a dozen or more police cars, their blue and red lights flashing and sirens blaring, heading toward the motel. They passed quickly beneath me, unable to see me hovering high above the roadway. At once, the afterburners kicked in and I accelerated through 200 mph, descending to about ten feet, and continued on. I flew along this way until about Santa Monica where I hit airborne traffic then I gently alighted back to the surface of the road and exited the highway.

I began to creep along city streets. Suddenly, porch lights began to illuminate sequentially, leading my way. This was marvelous as I no longer had to worry about navigation. I laughed uproariously with the realization that the city was once again conspiring in my favor helping me give the cops the slip. I traveled on deeper into the Westside following the illuminating porch lights and suddenly I was at Washington Boulevard in Culver City. I turned right and pulled into the left-hand lane. I accelerated rapidly.

Suddenly, there was a great bang and a loud thud and the car lurched to the right. Clearly, an officer had been dropped by helicopter onto the roof of the Mini. I jerked the wheel hard to the right to throw him off but he held on tight. I spun the wheel back to the left, accelerating still faster. Then I slammed on the brakes in hopes of throwing him over the hood but the bastard clung tight. It was then that I ran over the giant magnet LAPD had placed in the street. The car slowed quickly and lurched to a stop. I turned the key but it wouldn't start again. Obviously, the magnet had disabled the engine and battery.

It was then that I noticed the sharpshooter at the top of the block with his sight trained on my vehicle. I raised my hands in surrender. Then I noticed the bright light to my left as the television camera came into view. This was unfolding on live TV. The world would be watching this play out in real time. The abject, unspeakable humiliation was more than I could bear. I longed for death and would have taken my life right there in the car if I could have. For a brief moment, I considered stepping out of the Mini and rushing the cop at the top of the block in the hope that a well-placed bullet would end this horror once and for all. Still, I sat there frozen. A man came out of his house and stood on the porch, his hands in his pockets, watching me sit in the car with my hands in the air. He said nothing. I was utterly and physically exhausted. I wanted nothing more than out of the car and done with this nightmare at once. Clearly, I was surrendering. Why would they not remove me from the vehicle? Obviously, they thought I was a threat. How could I communicate to them that I was innocuous?

I reached over and picked up my phone and called Cynthia in Missouri. She could tell them. By now it was well past midnight there. She answered the phone sleepily. I told her that I was in the car somewhere on Washington Boulevard and that the police had their guns on me. I said there were news cameras all around and there was a cop on the roof of the car. She was understandably confused and certainly frightened, but she tried to talk me down and did a remarkable job of staying calm. After a few questions, she roughly determined my whereabouts and relayed the information to LAPD.

My hands were still in the air about half an hour later when a police car and an ambulance pulled up alongside me. Suddenly, I was snapped back to reality and I knew I was in a lot of trouble. To make matters worse, I was consumed by a fit of the giggles and could not stop laughing. I knew there was absolutely nothing humorous about my dire circumstances but I could not stifle my nervous laughter no matter how hard I tried. The more frightened and anxious I became, the more I giggled. When the officer asked what the problem was, I did not say it was the drugs or the wild hallucinations. I simply replied, "I can't stop laughing and I know there's absolutely nothing funny about this." The officer, having already spoken to Cynthia on the phone, knew the entire backstory already. "It looks like you ran out of gas," he said, flatly. "But obviously, there's something more going on here so we're going to bring you to the hospital to get checked out." He helped me from the vehicle and into the back of a waiting ambulance as a tow truck pulled up to haul my car away.

I was transported to Brothman Hospital in Culver City and kept for observation for a few hours. I don't know whose bright idea it was to release me into a neighborhood I was unfamiliar with, miles from home with no vehicle, not yet stabilized. Yet suddenly, I was on the street beneath the hot sun walking in the general direction in which I had last seen my car, psychotic and overwhelmed.

In my psychosis, I believed a new holiday had been avowed, that for one day, open season had been declared on Steven Slater. Loud voices called out from the shadows, threatening. Suddenly, every passerby bore a weapon and I was in danger of being bludgeoned, stabbed, or beaten. Hostile, angry crowds followed me everywhere I walked and I began to cry and hyperventilate. I ran, terrified, into the courtyard of an apartment building and began pounding on doors begging for someone to take me in and hide me. Finally, I hid beneath some bushes, holding perfectly still, not daring to breathe.

"Daddy, help me." I heard my son's voice, faint and weak floating into the courtyard from the distance. This made no sense. Brandon lived in Missouri. Still, I followed the voice out from under the bushes and around the Spanish courtyard of the pre-war building. "Help me," I heard again from above. I could not tell if the voice was coming from an upstairs apartment the roof. I walked out to the street and looked up.

"Daddy, help," I heard again, now from up the block. It was certainly Brandon's voice, clear in my ear, frightened and timid. At once, I set off in a dead run for the top of the block. When I arrived at the intersection, there was no one in sight in either direction. "No!" Brandon screamed out, panicked and terrified. Unable to tell which direction the scream had come from, I took off again down the main street, then rounded the corner onto Motor Street—a quiet, residential lane across from the MGM Studios.

Again, I heard Brandon's agonized and tortured scream but could not tell which house it came from. I ran up to the first home, climbed the steps to the porch, and tried the door. Again, Brandon screamed, this time from the house behind me. I turned and bolted across the street and pounded wildly on the front door. I tried several more houses before I realized he was locked in the trunk of a silver Mazda parked in a driveway halfway down the block. I had just ripped open the driver's door of the car and was searching frantically for the trunk release lever when a black and white police car rolled up alongside in the street and flashed its lights.

As is so often the case with psychosis, actual person-to-person, human interaction breaks the spell, at least for a moment. The officer called me over and asked me what I was doing. Suddenly, I was at a loss and didn't have an answer. The cop explained that they had received reports I was trying to break into homes. And now they had caught me red-handed breaking into a car. In short order, I was standing handcuffed with my hands behind my back and being lowered into the back seat of the police car.

Once inside, the psychosis returned full force. Suddenly, I was a contestant on a reality show that had gone too far. I was certain millions of viewers worldwide were watching this miscarriage of justice from their living rooms, enraged. I screamed to be let out. When the officers refused to pull over and discharge me alongside the freeway, I tried to break the window, slamming my head against the glass. I whipped myself into a fevered frenzy, screaming with rage and vitriol.

Once inside the Pacific Division station house, I screamed and wailed that they were making a huge mistake for which they would pay dearly. I became so violent and combative in the precinct that it was decided I should be transferred to a hospital. Back in the police car, I screamed and kicked and yelled and banged my head against the glass and the gate until blood ran from my forehead. Upon arrival at the hospital, I thrashed so badly that I pulled free of the officer's grip and plunged flat onto my face, handcuffed in the parking lot, and opened a large gash across my nose. The two officers lifted and carried me into the ambulance entrance of the hospital and set me down on a stretcher where I was quickly restrained, screaming and sobbing in full flight from reality.

I laid on a stretcher in a hallway, next to another patient, an older, homeless African-American man who had been brought in for chest pains. My psychosis ascribed voices to the doctors and nurses who worked on the man and I heard them say he was worthless and needed to be put down. So this was how it was. We had been brought to this place to be exterminated.

They would make it look like an overdose, they said. Momentarily, someone would shoot the man up with an obscene amount of cocaine which would trigger a heart attack. They laughed and snickered at their diabolical plan as they went about preparing the lethal dose. They would shoot him in the thigh and he would go quickly. I panicked upon hearing this, knowing not only would this be excruciatingly painful but the drug would not hit the bloodstream at all. The man would linger in terrible pain and possibly not succumb at all. In a brief moment of clarity, I knew what had to happen. I collected myself briefly and motioned to my young arresting officer who stood beside me, still guarding me after the events of the long day.

"Excuse me, sir. May I speak with you?" I asked softly, motioning him down to my face. "I heard everything that was just said and I understand what has to happen," I said with a heavy, resigned sigh. The officer looked anxious, confused. He looked away. "No, I understand," I continued, "but these people don't know what they're doing. They will hurt him terribly this way. Let me do it. He won't suffer," I said, as my eyes filled with tears. "It will be fast and he won't feel pain," I glanced sadly at the man sleeping quietly next to me. The officer's eyes grew wide and he shifted from foot to foot. "He won't suffer and no one will know it was me. They can believe it was you. Please, Let me do it. I beg you." A small tear formed in the corner of the young officer's eye and trickled down his cheek. He wiped it away, turned, and left the room.

At once, there was a loud, scraping scuffle on the roof.

"Your boy is gonna fly, Steven!" a man yelled down to me from above with a sardonic cackle. It was the doctor who, a moment ago, had been preparing the lethal shot to kill the man next to me. They had Brandon on the roof and were about to throw him to the parking lot below.

"Daddy! No!" Brandon screamed in terror.

I let out the most blood-curdling, inhuman, animalistic scream from the depths of my being and rose against the restraints with superhuman strength called up from every cell in my body. Suddenly, the stretcher was up on two wheels, tipping, tilting, tumbling, and I was falling onto my side, still strapped down as the young officer was catching me and righting me back up. The doctor's cruel laugh grew booming and more maniacal as Brandon's fevered scream grew still more panicked. Then he was almost out of earshot, softer, plaintive, almost begging. Then came the sickening, wet thud of his skull cracking against the pavement below. I went catatonic, numb, and I passed out cold.

CHAPTER 14

I had reached a level of psychosis where acute inpatient hospitalization was prescribed. Following yet another Thorazine shot, I was transferred to Kedren Acute Psychiatric Hospital in South Central Los Angeles to begin a 60-day stay.

Kedren was a classic cuckoo's nest, a loud and chaotic ward filled with downtrodden denizens of decay and decline. Patients were warehoused six to a room off blindingly-lit, white sterile hallways secured behind steel doors. Vacant-eyed zombies shuffled heavily in endless circles and violence was commonplace as psychotics battled demons unseen.

Each night, I laid beneath yet another County of Los Angeles blanket in the frigid, cavernous hospital room and listened to the discord of human angst as it played around me heavy and heartbreaking, the aching and heartrending, visceral devastation of suffering on a level otherwise unfathomable in a concentration unknown anywhere else on Earth. I turned my head to the cold and grimy wall and felt my heart shatter into a thousand pieces, my soul perishing in the captivity of each interminably long day kept out of the sunshine and warm summer sky beyond my reach.

Two fellow inmates, Miguel and Josue, and I formed a formidable trio who saw one another through the painful ordeal, leaning on one another for strength, dark humor, and perspective as the unending interment dragged on. Intense and fiery, with a lean and cutting build that caused my pulse to race when he was first pushed onto the ward with his hands cuffed behind his back, Miguel had been a Mexican soap opera leading man before the tumult of bipolar led to the gritty streets of L.A.'s Skid Row destitute and disheveled in virtual obscurity, a shadow of his dashing former self. Josue was a highly sensitive, empathic, and artistic high school dropout with a penchant for self-harm. Tears flooded my eyes when he revealed the 100 angry scars that marked his fleshy forearms, telling the tale of a life lived in unfathomable angst and sorrow. Each day following breakfast, we three would adjourn to the central courtyard and sit cross-legged on the gray-painted cement and share about our lives before mental illness and substance abuse had stolen our dreams and our freedom. We would lay prone on the warm cement and watch the cloud shapes pass overhead and talk out our plans upon our release. And if things had gotten particularly unbearable on the ward, we would fantasize plans for escape.

Each week, I met with my psychiatrist, Dr. Ana, a joyful and motherly Armenian woman who listened with patient bemusement as I told my rambling tales about the JetBlue fiasco, the violence with Scott, and the psychotic episodes I couldn't discern from reality anymore. I was extremely distraught and in a state of high anxiety. I wanted nothing more than to be back in the comfort of my own home managing my own affairs. I found being held against my will extremely traumatic and I begged anyone who would listen to help me in my bid to be released. I begged in earnest to be seen, to be heard for the autonomous, accomplished man of 42 years I was, but my agency had been stolen from me by a system that rendered me voiceless. Each day, I protested before the angry and aloof Russian head psychiatrist, Dr. Puskin, a brusque and dismissive man who made me anxious, and the puffy and self-aggrandized treatment team at my weekly "Patients' Rights Hearing," yet no one heard my impassioned plea.

About six weeks into my stay, I was called into Dr. Pushkin's office for a meeting to discuss plans for my upcoming discharge. With high hopes, I arrived excited about the prospects for my release. Dr. Ana began the meeting with a progress report stating that I had made great progress and was doing well. Dr. Pushkin could not be bothered to look up and continued to fuss with papers on his desk. Dr. Ana went on to ask me what my plans were upon discharge. I stated that I planned to return home as quickly as possible. She replied that she and Dr. Pushkin thought it wise that I stayed a few weeks longer, then went to rehab straight from the hospital. I said I didn't think that was necessary, that I had an AA group just down the street that I attended occasionally. This response seemed to piss off Dr. Pushkin who scoffed and slammed his pen down, then pushed himself backwards in his chair. Dr. Ana smiled sweetly and began to speak again.

I felt like I was in a classic game of "good cop, bad cop" as Dr. Ana went on to ask if I knew what a conservatorship was. I did not. She explained that it was similar to a temporary power of attorney where you asked a family member or someone you trusted to manage your medical decisions and financial affairs on your behalf.

"You are tired, you have been through so much," she continued. "You are so fortunate to have such a lovely family who comes to visit you. Wouldn't it be nice to let somebody help you for a little while?" she asked, concerned. Dr. Pushkin continued to slam and bang around the office behind me, making me considerably more nervous as the conversation continued and causing me to feel pressured to bring it to a close and bid a hasty retreat out of the office. Dr. Ana went on to explain that she had already spoken to Cynthia, who had agreed to serve as my conservator during my transition back to independent living. Cynthia would handle my medical decisions and bills for me so I could focus on my recovery. It would be merely a temporary arrangement, until I was a little bit stronger and ready to stand on my own. This was how they had helped Britney Spears and look how beautifully she was doing, she explained. Just as soon as I felt stronger and was ready to take back the reins, the conservatorship would be dissolved and I could resume independent living. This lie would cost me everything I ever owned and had worked so hard for in life.

Truth be told, it sounded wonderful. I was distracted, and I was falling behind and quite overwhelmed. On my desk at home stood a pile of overdue notices and unpaid bills. To sweeten the deal, Dr. Ana added, the County of Los Angeles would dispense a monthly allowance and a caseworker who would help manage all of this. Plus, the Public Guardian's Office maintained a police department, she explained, and Lord knew I now had enough ugly people in my world and could use a little extra protection.

Feeling relieved by the idea of a little help, I readily agreed to meet with a detective who would determine if this was a good idea for me. Dr. Pushkin slammed a file drawer behind me and stomped out of the office without further word.

Detective Solis was a taut and toned, young ex-LAPD officer who listened attentively with concern a week later as I described all that had occurred in the tumultuous months leading to my hospitalization. He agreed that I had bitten off more than I could chew with the dark people I had been running with, and felt that Public Guardian could help provide a level of protection I had been unable to provide for myself up until now. He enticed me further with the promise of a monthly stipend and I grew more intrigued. By the end of my conversation with this breathtaking man, I was sold. He told me I would need to appear in court in two weeks' time, and counseled me to relax in the safety of the hospital and continue to work on my recovery in the interim.

In the meanwhile, Dr. Puskin and Dr. Ana continued their hard sell for rehab, finally insisting that under California state law, they had the right to commit me to a program of up to six months involuntarily. I took this news with great duress, terrified I would never return to the beautiful home I longed for. My anxiety and heartbreak rose to unmatched levels with this decree and I cried incessantly day and night over this development and the seemingly endless delays that kept me locked away from my regularly scheduled life in progress.

The sun rose on day 42 of my confinement, but I was unable to rise from my bed. Numerous court delays had stretched my stay past the point of usefulness and my condition was now degrading once more much to the concern of my nurses, who correctly identified "cabin fever" as the culprit. I was literally suffocating spiritually and physically in my entrapment in the cold and dark, impersonal hospital filled with chaos and despair. For someone who based their identity and lifestyle on travel and independence, this captivation was the ultimate degradation. I was truly withering on the vine, and dying more each day.

I felt my spirit breaking as tears fell from my eyes in the dark and empty room. Quaintance, my heavy-set, black nurse with her weary, seen-it-all façade, entered the room and sat heavily on the nightstand beside me with a deep sigh and folded her arms over her ample chest. We sat in silence together for a minute or two, gazing toward the light shining through the opaque, frosted window.

At length, I spoke meekly. "They're killing me, Quaintance."

She considered silently for a moment, then leaned in toward me and whispered, "I have been doing this for many, many years, and this is wrong. You don't belong here, child. I told them they've got to get you out. We all have," she continued in a hushed, low voice.

"You're being tested like Job, child. Just like Job, you are. And you're gonna have to have the faith of Job to get through this. You have to dig deep inside you and find something to hold onto," she whispered earnestly. Believe that this will pass. You don't understand this now, but one day this will all make sense one day. But right now, you got to have faith."

I looked up into knowing eyes that had seen decades in the hospital just in time to see her look away and wipe away a single tear. And then, she broke into a soft, sweet hymn which floated lightly in the air and filled the room with healing song. Each note she raised up began to ease my weary heart as new, healing tears spilled from my eyes. Listening to Quaintance's ethereal song, I slumped back into the bed and I began to surrender at last. I asked God to deliver me from this ordeal. I confessed inwardly that I had no choice but to trust. I had truly exhausted myself in my fruitless efforts to prove myself. Perhaps acceptance would yield another way through this horrific affair.

In high school, I studied Spanish under one of those unforgettable teachers, Mrs. Levine, who ignited a passion for a subject and made the world come alive. She made arrangements with a UCLA professor to transport a handful of us to Ensenada for the weekend where we stayed with local families and worked an afternoon in an orphanage. I jumped at the invitation, imagining sundrenched beaches and bargain shopping on cobblestone streets.

When the van pulled up in front of the orphanage on Saturday morning, I was shocked and perplexed by the sight of the ramshackle, windowless building with crumbling stucco. An open front door led inside to a single large room with chipped, bare floors that showed years of wear. There were no overhead lights and the room was hot and stifling despite open windows. An assortment of well-worn cribs, weathered cots—and for the more fortunate older children, metal-framed twin beds with stained mattresses lined the room. Several joyful, stout women buzzed about cleaning industriously and although the place was quite worn, it was spotless.

Once we students regained our composure, chores were doled out efficiently. I was assigned to do some painting outside and tried to disguise the building's ugly, worn facade with a coat of perky yellow. After a couple hours of work in the beautiful Mexican sunshine and fresh sea breeze, I ventured back inside to join the others for a break, feeling renewed. A couple of the girls were sitting on the floor with a few of the toddlers playing with some handmade toys. The other girls were gathered around the cribs playing with the babies who cooed and gurgled with delight.

I walked up to a battered crib and peered down at the little one below. He was about six months old and terribly underweight, his little frame wrapped in a blanket, only his little head crowned with wispy, soft black hair was visible, half asleep. His head was cocked to the side and he stared vacantly ahead. I called out to him to no response, then drew my finger across his tepid cheek. He did not rouse. One of the orphanage women came by and explained in Spanish that his name was David and that he had been badly abused and did not respond to anyone.

I bent down and lifted him up and as I did so, his blanket fell down to expose his emaciated body. I shuddered when I saw the angry purple scars that abounded across his chest and abdomen where he had been burned repeatedly. Pulling him tighter, his head fell listlessly to the side as I lifted him, yet he just continued to stare off into space. I held his little head and directed his face towards mine. He looked vacantly over my shoulder, unable to meet my gaze or focus on anything in particular. What horrors had this child known and what kind of monster could have done such a thing to another human being, I wondered as tears began to roll down my cheeks. I swaddled him back up in his blanket and carried him over to a rickety folding chair in the corner where I sat with him in my arms and persisted in talking to him and caressing him in earnest.

I began to sing to him in hopes of eliciting some response for the broken boy. I remembered a song that had long brought me comfort, "Not While I'm Around" from Sweeney Todd. I began singing softly to him, "No one's gonna hurt you, no one's gonna dare, others may desert you, not to worry. Whistle, I'll be there." Transfixed by the wounds on the helpless baby's body, I sang the words over and over feeling helpless and useless against the magnitude of such evil. I spent the better part of the afternoon with the boy feeling as though time had stopped. Nothing existed but me and the wounded soul held tightly in my arms. By sunset, I had elicited a few furtive and aborted glances and a couple of hesitant and halting smiles. The orphanage women said it had been the most energy they had seen the boy display. I was profoundly moved and shaken by the encounter.

Now, two decades later, I lay broken and dispirited in the hospital room myself, as a young man was assisted into the room by two orderlies and laid on the bed where he pulled the covers up over his head and turned to the wall immediately. When called for group in the afternoon, he did not respond. A few hours later, the staff helped the young man from the bed and down the hall to the dining room where he took only a few small bites before again turning to the wall then being assisted back to bed. This routine went on for several days with the boy lying in the dark, his eyes closed, not responding to anyone. Something about the whole affair felt so familiar and I would study the boy from across the room trying to figure out why to no avail.

One day I stayed back from lunch to rest. As usual, the boy was brought back early and laid back on his bed with his eyes closed. I went about my routine of tidying up and found myself instinctively humming a long forgotten song. Absentmindedly I sang, "No one's gonna hurt you, no one's gonna dare…"

Suddenly, my eye caught a little movement in the darkened corner as the boy began to slowly and hesitantly turn away from the wall and look up toward the ceiling. I kept singing and soon the boy looked over in my direction, listening to me sing, regarding me with sad, vacant eyes. A few minutes later, a nurse entered the room, breaking the spell, and the boy quickly turned away and back to the wall for the rest of the night.

Encouraged by his response that morning, I began to sing to the boy anytime we were left alone in our room. I couldn't help but remember the impact Quaintance's beautiful voice had had on my spirit a few weeks earlier and I hoped that music could lift this boy's spirits as well. Soon, I caught a faint smile cross the young man's face as I sang one day, and I shared this news with Quaintance who told me to keep it up. Within a week, the shy, young man was up and about. Although he spoke no English, he made an effort to join in groups and meal times.

Then, at once he was gone, deported back to Mexico. I cried for the mysterious boy and the life of hardship ahead, and I could not help but think of another mysterious boy of many years ago in a small house in the hills high above Ensenada who had also touched my heart and with whom I had shared a sweet, secret song.

I was declared "Gravely Disabled" by judge Laura Hymnowitz at Los Angeles Mental Health Court 95A. Hearing myself described in such terms was humiliating and shocking. I prided myself on my exceptional abilities. I considered myself highly competent and I lived an extraordinary life. I traveled the world and maintained homes on both coasts. I held wide-ranging interests and considered myself a student of life, brimming with curiosity. I counted among my friends interesting and fascinating people. The term "Gravely Disabled" was wholly incongruous to how I regarded myself.

No longer would I be permitted to sign a legal document, travel outside of Los Angeles without permission, or drive a motor vehicle. I could no longer make decisions relating to my medical care or housing arrangements.

As drastic as all of this seemed, I was reminded that all it would take to dissolve the conservatorship was a letter from a psychiatrist attesting to my competence. It was truly my understanding that all of this was simply a necessary evil if I were to be released from the hospital anytime soon.

As terms of the conservatorship, I was immediately enrolled in a six-month program at the Victory House, an inpatient substance abuse rehab program for men in Burbank. Patients were housed in a converted motel in a residential neighborhood and transported each day to a classroom a few miles away. I was deeply depressed and highly upset about the additional delay in returning home. I hated the other, younger men who I found standoffish and boorish, and it didn't help that I was the only gay man in the facility.

Residents were kept on probation for the first 30 days of their stay and only permitted to travel between the living quarters and the treatment center. However, Cynthia, as conservator, made a stipulation that I was to remain on probation for the first four months. While my classmates were going out for pizza or shopping on the weekends, I was locked in my room like Rapunzel watching the world pass outside my window.

Shortly before my completion date, I heard from one of my old drug dealers up in Oxnard. Dino said he had some great stuff so I put in for a day pass from the rehab and jumped on the Amtrak and got a motel room. Dino arrived with a sketchy and skinny young man in tow, which foiled my plans. Although straight, Dino and I had fooled around regularly and I was looking forward to letting off some steam after being locked up in the hospital and rehab. I was pissed. The two men seemed anxious and edgy, bug- eyed and nervous.

Drugs in hand, I forgot about my return ticket and early curfew back at the rehab and within minutes, I shot up and was high as hell again. Dino and the mysterious stranger were tense. They kept running to the window and peeking out from behind the drapes at each sound from the parking lot.

Eventually, Dino and I argued over their erratic behavior and they left around 4 a.m. When I came back to Earth with the sunrise, I realized I was in big trouble. Not only had I gone AWOL from the court-ordered rehab, I had also broken the terms of the conservatorship by traveling out of Los Angeles County without the court's permission. I quickly cleaned up and checked out, and rode the train back to Burbank where I hung my head and walked back into the rehab, strung out and ashamed. At once, I was back on the dreaded probation phase.

My counselor called me into his office the next day. He had received a call from the Ventura County Sheriff's Office. A maid cleaning the motel room had found a pistol between the mattresses of the bed. The sheriff's department had traced the gun to a bank robbery in San Luis Obispo earlier that day. Dino and his little friend, captured by the motel surveillance video entering my room that night, had also been caught on the bank's surveillance video at the time of the robbery. I sat dumbfounded as the floor dropped out below me. Dino and the mysterious stranger had come directly to my room from the robbery and spent the night in hiding, then hid the evidence right under my nose, leaving me to take the fall.

And now, the cops in San Luis Obispo wanted to extradite me for questioning. I was terrified. There was no way out of this without getting caught up as an accessory. Wittingly or not, I had aided and abetted a bank robbery and helped discard evidence. I had harbored fugitives. There was no way this could end with me a free man. This would end with me either behind bars or in a hospital for the criminally insane. I was told to sit tight in the rehab while the investigation continued. Under no circumstances was I to leave the program or I would be transported directly to jail.

I sat in abject terror for the better part of the next two weeks, not daring to leave the building. Thankfully, further examination of the motel surveillance video established my alibi by placing me checking in at the motel at the time of the bank robbery one hundred miles away. Furthermore, my "Gravely Disabled" status also worked in my favor as I was determined not to have the mental capacity to provide useful testimony. A week later, Dino and his gang were busted for the bank robbery and a massive methamphetamine distribution operation, and their faces were flashed across the evening news.

I finished an extra month of rehab and moved into an apartment in North Hollywood.

CHAPTER 15

Ensconced in the new apartment, the first order of business was taking back the reins back on my personal affairs. Under the terms of conservatorship, I was required to see a psychiatrist regularly. I assumed I could kill two birds with one stone by getting the new psychiatrist to perform an evaluation for the courts, attesting to my competence. Cynthia, as conservator, selected the psychiatrist.

I arrived at the office of Dr. Pantea Farhadi at Cedars-Sinai and took a seat in the well-appointed waiting room. Forty-five minutes past our appointment time, she greeted me and ushered me in. She explained that she had been on the phone with Cynthia gathering information about my case. Immediately, I felt suspicious and wary.

From the start it was clear she had little interest in my situation and had been prejudiced by what she heard prior to meeting me. I said that I was looking for help with ending my conservatorship and in need of a psychiatric evaluation for the courts. Dr. Farhadi was uninterested and dismissive, and explained that no psychiatrist would involve herself in such an affair without first treating a client for at least six months. I was shocked and incredulous, as my public defender and my doctors at Kedren had explained that this would be simply a formality. We argued, which set the tone for the remainder of our working relationship. I left angry and frustrated, and insistent upon finding a new psychiatrist.

Dr Farhadi charged me $300, due in cash, at the end of the session which would be her standard rate for the weekly sessions we established. This was highly unethical knowing that I was prohibited from engaging in financial transactions while conserved.

To add insult to injury, the payments were to come from my personal savings. The stipend account from the Public Guardian's office was either never set up, or the funds were being diverted elsewhere, leaving me to foot the bill each week for what amounted to extortion and abuse.

Dr. Farhadi insisted that if I remained compliant with her demands and so-called care, she would recommend the conservatorship be dissolved at my next scheduled hearing six months away. I felt betrayed and violated by this turn of events, and utterly helpless.

To make matters worse, the doctor advised me that I did not enjoy the benefit of patient-client confidentiality. Anything I reported in session could be reported back to Cynthia. I became mistrustful and resentful when I began to hear back from Cynthia things that I had shared in confidence with Dr. Farhadi.

It was becoming clear that under the terms of conservatorship, I had been rendered voiceless, stripped of my agency and free will. I had clearly made a huge mistake by acquiescing to this ill-advised arrangement.

My beautifully decorated home was my crowning accomplishment. Four bedrooms, elegantly appointed, abounded with tasteful furnishings and included my grandparents' bedroom set from pre-war Germany and an extensive collection of Scandinavian decorative art pieces my mother painted over the years. An elaborate dining room set housed heirloom china and silver while treasured family photographs in ornate frames cluttered every surface.

When I was sent to treatment, I agreed to letting Cynthia rent out my home while I was away. The rental income was to be deposited into my savings account each month. My furniture and personal belongings would be placed in storage and a portion of the rental income would pay for the unit each month.

Yet I never saw a single deposit into my account, nor a payment to a storage company. When first questioned, Cynthia told me that she was paying the storage bill directly from her own account and that the rental income was being used for school expenses for Brandon, now a college freshman, an expense I could not very well begrudge. However, when pressed for the name and location of the storage company, Cynthia could not provide the information and finally stopped answering my calls entirely. It became clear that there was no storage and that my belongings had been sold or discarded.

When I addressed this concern with Dr Farhadi, she always vowed to follow up with Cynthia but was not forthcoming either.

I never received an accounting of the whereabouts of the contents of my home. It was as if a lifetime had simply vanished overnight.

I confided my growing concerns to my general practitioner. He gave me a referral for another psychiatrist who he thought could help. I made an appointment for a psychiatric evaluation with a new psychiatrist at Brothman Hospital in Culver City. I told Cynthia about the upcoming appointment and she tipped off Dr. Farhadi. On the day of the appointment, I signed in and took a seat to wait in the waiting room. I was ushered into the examination room and hopped up on the examination table where I sat for an unusually long time. At length, a security guard and a doctor from the emergency room came and told me I was being placed on an involuntary hold for psychiatric observation.

When I questioned why, I was told it would be explained in the ER. I was escorted to a bed in the emergency room where I was sat angry and confused for the rest of the afternoon. None of the emergency room staff could understand why I was there and all were infuriated by my treatment.

Later in the evening, I was transferred to the psych ward where Dr. Farhadi finally came to see me. She told me that Cynthia had requested my hospitalization. By requesting an evaluation from another doctor, I had proved too much to handle. I was infuriated and grew enraged. Other than having the audacity to advocate for my own needs, there was clearly nothing wrong with me. Dr. Farhadi had no choice but to release me at once.

Sentencing me to an afternoon in the psych ward had been an attempt to put me back in my place. It sought to send a message that I had gotten too big for my britches and was intended as a punishment. I should have brought up malpractice charges at the time but I mistakenly believed it to be a miscommunication and foolishly assumed everyone to be working in my best interests.

When I first fell under custody of the Public Guardian's office, I had the option of selecting a court-appointed guardian with no vested interest in my case. However, when this option was presented, Cynthia told me a disingenuous yet brilliant lie that I fell for hook, line, and sinker. Cynthia convinced me the state would levy my home and sell it, then use the proceeds to pay my expenses during the duration of my conservatorship. Terrified of losing my most prized possession, I would have done anything to prevent that from happening.

At this point, a well-mechanized process was stripping me of my autonomy, agency, and my assets. Not only was Dr. Farhadi basically extorting $1,200 dollars a month in cash, thousands of dollars were being siphoned from my investments and savings directly into Cynthia's accounts in Missouri, despite the fact that the law prohibited our finances from commingling. Instead, she helped herself to what she felt entitled to from my funds.

Unbeknownst to me, Cynthia flew to California and petitioned the courts to dissolve my long-standing trust and to create a new document, claiming it had become too cumbersome to manage my affairs as it stood. The courts allowed Cynthia to remove my name from my bank accounts and deposit $150 on a debit card for my use each week.

After the first month, Cynthia stopped depositing money onto the debit card, leaving me penniless and destitute. Thankfully, my friends saw what was happening and picked me up each week to take me to dinner and the movies or grocery shopping, buying me basic necessities. It was degrading and humiliating having to call and beg each week for my money, which Cynthia always promised was on the way. Each week, she blamed it on a clerical error at the bank, making up elaborate stories about her noble and heroic efforts to fix the issue.

Cynthia was my high school sweetheart. We shared more history than any two people. We laughed at inside jokes and could finish one another's sentences. And yet, there was no denying the glaring evidence that she was abusing me at every turn.

Caught in vacillation between the aching need to believe and the encroaching reality of what was, I could not find my footing. Everything I once believed began to fall away and I felt truly and terrifyingly alone, lost in a world I could not make sense of. Torn between a sense of loyalty and male pride, I couldn't share my misgivings with anyone. So I suffered my embarrassment and shame in desperate isolation and fear. What I could not see at the time was that I had selected a narcissist to be my protector and conservator.

Marijuana had just been legalized when I moved into the apartment in North Hollywood. I watched the trendy hipsters come and go from the dispensary across the street each night, looking no worse for the wear, and I decided to give pot another try. After the first toke, I realized I had blown my sobriety and figured I may as well go all out. In no time, I was standing on my dealer's doorstep, buying an 8-ball of meth.

Soon enough, I was hiding in the closet of my apartment hearing voices and footsteps just a few feet away outside the closet door in my bedroom. I felt the floor flex and shake as the shadowed figure moved about the room in search of me, intent on harm. I didn't dare breathe, hiding beneath a laundry pile in stark terror. I must have remained captive in the apartment for a long time because eventually, two LAPD officers knocked at the door conducting a welfare check.

By the time the officers arrived I was desperate for help. With kindness and compassion, they sized up the situation immediately. They calmed me and asked me a few questions. I kept apologizing over and over although I wouldn't say for what, despite the obvious. They escorted me down a back stairwell affording me privacy and drove me to the station house where I was interviewed by an understanding police psychiatrist who determined I needed help, not jail that night.

The officers asked me if I was willing to go to the hospital. I was exhausted and weary and could not bear the thought of another night of aching loneliness under the suffocating weight of depression alone in the apartment. I agreed readily with gratitude. I cried softly in the back seat of the police car as we raced down the deserted 405 freeway in the pre-dawn hours toward Brothman, crushed by guilt and remorse for the stupid decision that had brought me back to this shameful predicament after so much progress and hard work.

Given my now impressive dossier of arrests and hospitalizations, the treatment team was not inclined to let me return to the apartment at all this time. The recommendation was that I be sent to a board and care facility at Metropolitan State Hospital.

I was horrified. Kedren had been absolutely ghastly. The Brothman staff assured me that the board and care was a lower level of care and that I would be permitted to come and go freely throughout the day. They described it more like an assisted living facility for patients with developmental disabilities or going through temporary challenges. I recoiled at the thought. I was adamant that this was a step in the wrong direction, that restricting me further would only traumatize me and cause me to spiral into deeper depression. Yet conserved as I was, I had no say in the decision. The doctor's recommendation became the court's order, and I was transferred despite my objections.

Metropolitan was a 162-acre compound consisting of a modern high-rise hospital surrounded by a collection of rambling Tudor buildings in various states of disrepair or abandonment. The hospital was the subject of a 1976 documentary which exposed the widespread practices of involuntary drugging, the barbaric overuse of electroshock therapy, and the heavy-handed use of restraints. Crumbling, vacant facades dotted the campus and spoke of the hospital's checkered past in which hundreds of patients died in botched experiments and lobotomies. It was an absolute hall of horrors and my blood ran cold when the van first pulled through the gate to deliver me to my new home.

One look at the filthy and rundown facility turned my stomach.

Drugged-out schizophrenics roamed the halls and drug use ran rampant. My first phone call was to the Board of Health to file a complaint about the squalid conditions. The lobby was filled with threadbare sofas littered with zombies and downtrodden ghosts who had given up on life, their spirits broken. Many patients could have returned to normal living years ago, but had made peace with the astounding mediocrity. I was repelled, adamant that this would not be my lot in life, and resolved to fight with everything I had to get away from this death camp in short order.

I met with my new treatment team and immediately voiced my concerns. I made it clear that I could not thrive in this macabre environment. I made an impassioned plea to join outside activities and my counselor helped me sign up for an outpatient substance abuse program, and I quickly enrolled at nearby Cerritos College.

On Saturdays, I rode the Metrolink train and a subway and bus to West Hollywood to attend a Crystal Meth Anonymous meeting. The journey took two and a half hours each way but provided a much needed escape from the noise and tumult of the facility. I started working with a sponsor and soon, I built up a little clean time and found some hope once more, preparing for the next Conservatorship hearing a few months away.

An old friend with whom I had gotten sober in New York reached out during my third month at Metropolitan. Brad Lamm had founded a luxury rehab in Los Angeles specializing in trauma-informed treatment and helped a number of our mutual friends find lasting sobriety. The campus was set high in the Hollywood Hills and residents were housed in a number of former celebrity homes with access to fitness trainers, personal chefs, and a grotto pool. Yoga, equine therapy, and a host of alternative healing methods blended nicely with traditional 12-step work to create an effective treatment plan. I was transferred to Breathe Life Healing Center for a four-month stay, greatly relieved to escape the horrors of Metropolitan.

The team at Breathe convinced Cynthia to allow me to part with Dr. Farhadi and work with Dr. Morris, a psychiatrist at the Los Angeles

Gay and Lesbian Center. Dr. Morris was highly experienced with conservatorship cases and the Mental Health Court. I cried tears of relief at our first meeting as he laid out a plan to get me back in good standing with the court and off conservatorship shortly.

I graduated Breathe and moved into a charming little house at the corner of Laurel Canyon and Fairholm, just a few blocks up from Sunset Boulevard, adjacent to the ruins of the Houdini mansion and a stone's throw from Chateau Marmont. The beautiful cottage sat behind a high wall and had once been the residence of Carole Lombard. Lombard had bought the walled home to afford privacy during her affair with Clark Gable and had thrown legendary Hollywood parties entertaining around the piano in the bay- windowed living room.

I shared the home with my fashion executive roommate, Matthew, some fun millennials, and a wacky and loveable Pointer Sister. It was a great crew and always loads of fun. The house had a mischievous, impish energy and there was no question that Carole was always about.

Matthew and I would sit up in the late hours and watch the closet door swing open and closed by itself as Carole stirred. One night shortly after I moved in, Matthew placed a ring in a jewelry box and set it inside the closet. Within minutes, the ring disappeared from inside the box. By morning, the ring had been returned safely to its place inside the box in the closet. The next night, we sat in wide-eyed wonder as the closet opened itself slowly and my TWA flight attendant wings disappeared from on top of the dresser. Then the closet slowly swung closed. As before, the wings mysteriously returned to the dresser top by morning.

Much intrigued, I checked out a biography about Carole Lombard, which I quickly devoured. Much to my surprise, I learned that Carole was killed in the crash of a TWA DC-3 that flew into a mountain while departing Las Vegas as she raced home to this very house and her husband's side after a radio appearance in 1942. A coin toss decided that Carole, her mother, and a family friend would take TWA Flight 3 from Chicago to Burbank via Las Vegas. Carole's mother considered the number three unlucky.

I realized at once why Carole was displeased. To make peace, Matthew and I walked down to Hollywood Boulevard and found a glamorous black and white photo of the home's former owner, which we framed and placed on the mantle in the living room. I asked her for her forgiveness on behalf of TWA and for her permission to stay in her beautiful home. Peace was made and the duration of the stay was a harmonious one.

Sadly, Cynthia failed to pay the rent on my behalf and I was unceremoniously evicted from the storied home.

My friends Jack and Adam had just closed on a house and Adam and I went for a celebration dinner. On the way out of the restaurant, we stopped into a Pier One to get ideas for their new place. Realizing Adam had never seen my house, I punched my address into my cell phone to pull up a picture off the Internet. What came up took my breath away. My house was listed for sale at $650,000 on Zillow.

The room spun and I had to steady myself on a display rack. "What is it?" Adam asked. Without speaking, I handed him the phone. Adam looked at the listing, then handed the phone back and said steadily, "Call her now."

I tried to gather myself as we walked out of the store and across the parking lot. I felt like I had been punched in the stomach. For months, I had been trying to deny the obvious, to hold the glaring truth at bay. Friends glazed over when I protested and defended Cynthia despite the obvious and mounting evidence. Now, I felt as though the ground had opened wide and was in a free fall. I was devastated, shocked, and beginning to feel rage.

Once inside the car, I dialed Cynthia's number in Missouri. I was incensed and it took all I had not to explode when she answered. "Is there something I need to know?" I snapped. Cynthia sounded disoriented and confused. I had woken her.

"My home is not for sale," I seethed. She woke up quick.

She gave me a story about trouble with the renters. The renters whose names I had never heard, whose money I had never seen. The renters who obviously didn't exist.

"My house is not for sale," I stated again, emphatically.

Finally, she began to sob. "You need to talk to your son," she cried out, then hung up.

I looked at Adam dumbfounded and relayed the conversation. "What in the world could she have meant by 'You need to talk to your son?'" I wondered aloud, mystified. We drove back to Jack and Adam's apartment bewildered, trying to make sense of the baffling conversation.

I was sitting in an AA meeting when I received a text message from Adam. *Call me*, it said. I stepped outside and dialed. "You're not gonna like this," he said. He had run a title search on my house. He then texted me a screenshot of a title transfer in which the deed to my home had been transferred out of my name and into that of my son a week prior. A second transfer showed the sale to yet another owner.

I felt the breath leave my chest and a knife plunge through my heart. The betrayal left me reeling. Cynthia had lied to me when I tried to stop this from happening a few weeks earlier.

Brandon had done this. My son. There were no words for the shock and horror of the moment as I tried to wrap my head around the disingenuity of the very people I entrusted my life to. My world collapsed in that instant and my heart shattered. Although devastated, I was above all, deeply concerned for my son. This was not a speeding ticket or a fight at school. This was a very serious crime committed by my child. I prayed for guidance and the presence to be a good father in these very serious circumstances. I called Cynthia. She didn't answer. I left a tearful message sharing my disappointment and heartbreak, as well as my anger. But above all, I spoke of my concern for our son.

Then I called Brandon. He answered. I tried to keep it light. I began the conversation by telling him that I loved him first and foremost. I went on to say that I was very concerned by what I had learned, but reassured him that I wasn't angry, only hurt and very confused. I told him I believed there had been some huge misunderstanding. I told him what he had done was wrong, that he had committed a crime, but that I was certain we could sort it out, together. I told him he had to make this right but committed to helping him do so. Brandon was distracted, in and out of the conversation. He was defensive and evasive.

"You gave me that house. Don't you remember? Everyone was there."

Yet when pressed for details of this ever-so-generous gift, he could offer none.

"I think I would remember such a generous gift," I replied incredulously. "I mean, where would I sleep if I gave you the roof over my head?" I countered.

He had no reply. He was impatient and rushed and hurried off the phone, promising to call back shortly. To no surprise, he never called back and my calls were met with voicemail.

Brandon answered three days later. He sounded groggy, his words slurred. He was irritable and put out by the whole affair.

"I told you, you gave me the house!" he snapped. "You don't remember anything." His insolence and disregard angered me. I quickly changed my tactic.

"You need to understand something right now," I hissed. "What you have done is a crime. You have a choice, you can answer to me, or you can answer to the authorities. Right now, I can still help you, but if this goes to the cops, it's out of my hands and there is nothing I can do for you."

Again, he gave me his song and dance about my having given him the home.

"Fine, maybe I did," I said. "Then where is the title transfer? You get a receipt when you buy an appliance or a sweater. Certainly you have the paperwork from me giving you a house." At this, he was stumped. He began to stammer and stutter. There was a clatter and a clang and a muffled curse as he dropped the phone to the floor. A moment later, he was back on the line.

"I'm tired. I need to lay down," he complained in a slurred voice. Apparently, this was more than he could be bothered with.

I took a deep breath and said a silent prayer. Then I said one of the most difficult things I have ever uttered. I began deliberately and calmly, "Let me make this easier for you. You've made a huge mistake and you need to fix this. I want to help you, but you are making this extremely difficult." I continued, "You have a lot to think about and I'm sure you're overwhelmed. I'm going to give you 30 days to decide what you're going to do. If I do not hear from you in 30 days, I'm taking this to the police. At that point there will be nothing I can do to help you." I finished with, "The choice is yours."

My generous offer was met by Brandon hanging up on me once more.

CHAPTER 16

I was staying in a motel in the Valley awaiting a bed in a transitional housing and substance abuse program. Cynthia was still playing games with my finances, often withholding my weekly $150 allowance. Now, I was out of cash and facing eviction from the motel in the morning. I left her yet another message which went ignored as usual.

I called Brandon. The conversation started awkwardly and quickly went south. I explained the situation and asked him for $1,000 to tide me over until I could get into the program. He refused. I grew angry, insisting that it was my money in the first place. He replied that I was an embarrassment and that he was entitled to that money and the house for what he had put up with over the years. I was shocked, devastated, and heartbroken. I could barely speak. Never had Brandon spoken to me cruelly. Nor had he ever indicated that he harbored such feelings. He had always been concerned, compassionate, and kind to me.

Pushing the hurt aside, I went at it again, explaining that I would have to sleep in an alley behind a nearby 7-Eleven if he would not help me. I explained that a storm was due in overnight. He told me that wasn't his problem. His heartless decree left me reeling. I hung up and paced the room in heart-wrenching agony. I laid down and cried through most of the night. I stayed awake in fear and dread of the day to come.

The rain was falling the next morning when I hoisted my tote bag onto my shoulder and stepped out into the cold. I walked down Reseda Boulevard and turned to face the alley behind the 7-Eleven and a tire shop. I was frightened, consumed by shame, and I could not will my feet to take me into the soggy alley lined with dumpsters, discarded tires, and water-logged rubbish. At length, I moved slowly inward and past the back door to the convenience store, expecting someone to jump out and chase me away for trespassing. With heavy sadness and resignation, I found a discrete spot against a soggy telephone post and a cinder block wall, and sat down on the wet and grimy pavement, my back to the pole, and hid my head in my knees as the frigid rain fell hard against my back.

For the better part of two hours I sat shivering in shame and humiliation. I had never before known such vulnerability and fear. Each car passing down the alley made me jump. Exposed to the elements with nowhere to hide, I began to panic. Unrelenting fear coupled with utter exhaustion left me jagged and jumpy. Just as it had a year earlier on the streets of Hollywood, my psyche became overloaded and mania began to manifest. Suddenly, I had to escape the mounting terror. I snatched up my bag and started down Reseda Boulevard, growing ever more frightened of the unrelenting traffic and bright city lights. My anxiety and panic ramped to higher levels. The incessant pounding of stinging rain against my face became tortuous. I turned east at Ventura and took cover in the Galleria until the storm passed.

It was mid-morning as I passed the vacant storefront on Magnolia Boulevard, where the construction crew was hard at work. I stopped dead in my tracks when I saw the table saw in the center of the room. At once, I knew its purpose. In a few short hours, work would be finished on the house of horrors where I would meet my demise. These were the men who would carry it out. Standing still and deathly quiet, I closed my eyes. I could hear their gruff voices inside as they spoke of their plan. I heard the rage and derision in their voices filled with scorn. At once, I ran for the Red Line, tripped down the steps, and onto the first passing train.

I could still hear them, hard at work in the storefront. I heard the agile saw as it nimbly sliced through wood and metal. Their sardonic laughter echoed through my head even as the train traveled deep through the mountainside. I had made fools of them by escaping and I must pay. I overheard the plot as it unfolded. They laid it all out in sickening, vivid detail, for my review. My tormentors had studied me and researched me well. They knew me intimately, my innermost fears and my traumas. At this very moment, they were positioning themselves throughout the city, ready to snatch me up as I passed by, terrified and unaware.

A suicide note would be leaked to the press. But in actuality I was destined for a lifetime of backbreaking manual labor in a Peruvian rock quarry beneath the unrelenting sun—that was, if I survived the journey. Suddenly, I heard one voice above the others, as he explained precisely how it would all play out. "Everyone knows he's terrified to fly. Scared shitless of turbulence. So we take 'em up and shake him up good. Real bad shit, like free falls, till he loses his shit good," the man explained gruffly. "And since he's such a big fuckin' druggie, let's give him what he likes eh? Shoot him up with so much shit he has a fuckin' heart attack in the middle of it all. Then ya throw a few poisonous snakes down the aisle and livestream that shit, Mr. Celebrity. We'll use a JetBlue of course and we'll get one with an engine out that can't get over the mountains. He'll see the ridge coming up long before he hits it." This was punctuated by the loud "ding" of a Fasten Seat Belt sign blinking on and the cackle of a dozen maniacal voices breaking into riotous laughter as cold, stark terror overtook me and desperate tears welled in my eyes.

When the doors opened at Vermont/Beverly, I jumped up and burst out of the train and up the stairs, sobbing hysterically. Once on the street, I looked quickly from left to right, lost and confused. I ran full speed through the throngs of people on the street, expecting someone to lunge forth and grab me. Suddenly, I realized I had to end my life before this ghastly plot came to pass.

I ran into a diner. In tears of desperation, I begged the woman behind the counter for a knife. Her eyes grew wide, and she quickly walked away and into the kitchen where she spoke low and urgently with the cook. They stood together regarding me solemnly, and I turned and walked back onto the street. The voices continued taunting and tormenting me, as they rehashed the diabolical plan. Over and over again the chime of the seat belt sign dinged in my head, ratcheting me into further panic and terror.

Just ahead, I spotted an antique store. Out of my mind with anguish and anxiety, I burst through the door. The store was empty. I had to do this at once. I picked up a heavy porcelain vase and regarded it for a split second. Directly ahead stood a large, ornate china cabinet filled with delicate stemware and plates. Without a second thought, I smashed the heavy vase down into the glass doors of the cabinet. The sound of shattering glass ricocheted through the store as a cascade of shards rained down onto the floor like silvery sleet. I reached down and picked up a particularly sharp piece of broken stemware and quickly slashed it firmly across my left wrist. Instantaneously, a burst of bright red broke out across my wrist and began to pulse and spurt across the floor. A man shouted from across the store and I dropped the glass. I looked up but saw no one. Desperately, I dropped to the floor and picked up a piece of the jagged, broken pottery and lifted it to my right wrist. In a frenzy, I began to saw and hack at the tough skin of my wrist. Soon, I drew blood again.

I threw the shard down and ran from the store and out onto Beverly Boulevard where I threw myself down onto the pavement as traffic skidded to a stop. Concerned passersby began to gather on the sidewalk, calling out. I knew I had not lost my pursuers. They would catch up to me momentarily. Sitting upright in the middle of the street, I began to peel back the skin over my veins with my fingers in an attempt to hurry the bleeding.

A siren broke my reverie. Suddenly, a police officer was standing over me. I was incomprehensible, and convinced he was part of the plot. In short order, an ambulance was arriving on the side street, and the officer was explaining that I had a choice of vehicle in which to ride. I chose the ambulance, still convinced, however, that it was part of the conspiracy. Within a few minutes I was once again at Cedars-Sinai Emergency.

When I came to, following my requisite Thorazine shot, I was handed a carbon copy of my admittance paperwork.

You are being placed in the psychiatric facility because it is the opinion of professional staff that as a result of a mental disorder, you are a danger to yourself. We feel this is true because you said, "I am seeing a lot of people and hearing other people's thoughts, life is crazy—I can't keep up with it. I don't feel safe." You were in a manic state, afraid you would cut yourself or hang yourself as you have tried to do in the past. You have a history of multiple suicide attempts and hospitalizations and you are unable to contract for safety. You are unable to think, speak, act rationally due to hearing voices and seeing things. You are homeless, unable to negotiate the community, fend for yourself, meet your basic life needs. You will be held for a period up to 72 hours.

I was at the mercy of the psychiatric care team once more.

I was truly out of options when I was released from the hospital. With no money and no help from Brandon and Cynthia, I had no safe place to return to. I was referred to a homeless shelter.

The smell of urine hovered in the hundred degree air and newspapers fluttered on the breeze as I walked tentatively and terrified up the street with my see-through, plastic patient's belongings bag. Downtrodden and disenfranchised men sat on milk crates in front of the brick building smoking crack openly. I was accosted from all sides by drug dealers purveying their cheap and plentiful wares as gang members on low bicycles circled the streets, keeping a sharp eye on the goings-on of the Skid Row neighborhood.

I entered the building and checked in with a man behind a heavy bulletproof window and was assigned a top bunk in a 4th floor dormitory housing 20 men and sharing a common bathroom. I passed through a metal detector and rode the elevator up.

I stepped out onto the 4th floor. Suddenly the deafening sound of automatic gunfire reverberated from the street below. There were screams and shouts and the unmistakable wail of a man in agony. A heavy silence fell. I ran to the window but all I saw was the inner courtyard. A man cried out heavy and labored from the street below, "We're dying here!"

I laid on my bunk in tears listening to the sound of sirens and police radios from the street below as the victims were removed and life went on, on Skid Row.

Anxious to flee the dreary and dispiriting shelter, I rose early, showered in the communal facility, and walked down the street to the Los Angeles Mission for church service and breakfast each morning.

Services were generally spirited and joyful, heavy on live music, and I found my faith renewed in the uplifting sermons. I proclaimed my long tarnished faith in altar calls and invitations to prayer and came away feeling renewed despite my dire straits. Following church service, the doors were opened to the canteen, and I would take my place in line for oatmeal or cream of wheat ladled out from giant vats, then take a seat at a long communal table seating 100 or more.

Most of the diners were homeless African-American men living on the streets of Skid Row. A sense of gratitude and humility pervaded the table and I found the experience both heartwarming and humbling. I struck up a very special friendship with a former Black Panther, who became my confidante and protector. We had many deep and profound conversations in which we learned much about one another and our very disparate life experiences. I learned about the streets and the struggles of the men who called them home. Their stories of hardship and fortitude were heartbreaking and left me frustrated and filled with anger at the injustice they faced each day.

From the Mission, I generally headed to MacArthur Park, where I spread a blanket beneath a palm tree and enjoyed the fresh air and sunshine and a long nap. In the afternoon, I would rouse myself and walk to the Central Library where I would make myself comfortable and read for an hour or two, then log on to Facebook and check in with friends. Then, I would head back to the Mission for another church service followed by dinner and fellowship.

Although I faced the most daunting and dire circumstances

imaginable, I found my Skid Row experience to be a compelling and enriching foray into humanity and faith. It brought newfound perspective and restored my gratitude. Walking and living among folks who cultivated dignity and humanity despite imaginable poverty and neglect was both inspiring and profoundly humbling. I came away from the experience with a newfound appreciation for the beauty and resilience of the human spirit. I was that much more thankful when a bed opened up in a transitional housing project in the San Fernando Valley. I headed to Tarzana Treatment Center with a grateful heart.

CHAPTER 17

At a year sober, I moved to San Diego with my sights set on a little place South of the Border. I fell in love with a three-bedroom house on the side of a hill with a large balcony overlooking a lush valley in a humble and quaint colonial about 15 miles east of Tijuana. The house was painted a cheerful and bright ocean blue with beautiful tile floors. The shade of a giant peppertree and a cool sea breeze kept the house cool and comfortable. It was idyllic.

The one drawback, however, was an arduous and unpredictable four-hour commute to my job at SeaWorld San Diego made challenging by the whims of the U.S. Border Patrol and the mounting tensions owing to the political climate.

One evening, I hitched a ride with a coworker to the border crossing at San Ysidro, adjacent to downtown Tijuana, and crossed over just after dark. As it was my first time crossing at San Ysidro instead of my usual Otay Mesa checkpoint further east, I decided to take the opportunity to visit downtown Tijuana and the famous Revolucion District renowned for its bars and nightlife.

I felt the rush of the bright, garish neon lights of the city. I soon found myself lost in the heat and heady sway of blaring music in Mexico's gay nightlife mecca perusing the abundant offering of bars and clubs. In no time, I was chatted up by an attractive Mexican man who asked if I wanted to find a motel and party. He was hot as hell and

I was thrilled by the proposition. We went around the corner where I rented us a $20 room for the night.

Once behind closed doors, we quickly undressed. He was exquisite. He pulled out a meth pipe, and took a hit. He was passionate and virile, and when he left two days later, he stole my phone.

I was dehydrated and strung out, still wearing my work uniform when I tried to cross the border back to the United States to make a quick run to the Cricket Wireless store to replace my stolen phone.

I was coming down from the strong Mexican meth when I approached the counter, an owl-eyed wreck, and handed the Customs agent my passport. He looked at me then down at his screen, and back at me quizzically. "You doing alright there? What were you doing in Mexico?" he asked sternly. I replied that I lived in Maclovio Rojas and that I was headed up to do some shopping.

"Apparently, you missed work and your friend reported you missing," he continued to my horror.

He went on to explain that I would need to answer some additional questions in an office across the hallway. Once inside, I was instructed to take a seat against the wall next to some very anxious and frightened Mexican men.

After a few minutes, I was called up to a counter where I was interviewed by two more officers. They asked me some questions about my whereabouts for the last 24 hours and I explained that it had been nothing more than an irresponsible weekend on Revolucion. The officers informed me that the FBI and Mexican authorities had been alerted and that jurisdiction fell to the FBI who would determine whether they wished to interview me or simply hand me over to the Customs and Border Patrol at this point. I was told to return to the lobby while they called the FBI to sort it out. After a few minutes, they told me I could go but that I would need to have my friends resolve the missing person's report or I would be pulled aside for secondary screening each time I tried to cross the border.

I thanked them for their concern and got out of the office as quickly as possible. I headed to the Cricket store to buy a new phone.

Once back over the border, I headed right back to the motel in hopes of meeting another dark-eyed stranger with a pocket full of meth, as the demon of addiction had been released all over again.

The Motel Rosado did not disappoint. As I approached, I was propositioned by a rugged young hustler who introduced himself as Armando. He asked if I were getting a room and did I want to party. Of course I did, and we were getting undressed in a room in no time. Armando laid out an arsenal of drugs like I'd never seen before. The very best Mexican products. I told him I didn't have enough money for a spread like that. He said not to worry and we settled on a surprisingly reasonable figure for favors and a fuck.

Armando was a generous man and soon I was flying higher than ever before. He asked if I wanted to throw a little room party, maybe invite some of his friends over. Blasted as I was, I was down for anything. He made a few calls. A short time later, there was a knock at the door. Armando invited in a shy and gentle young man and a tough looking middle-aged woman. The woman was brusque and made me nervous. She was clearly the young man's madame. She said she needed to make a call and asked to use my phone, and stepped out into the hall with it. Armando, the young man, and I all got higher and began to fool around together.

Unbeknownst to me, the woman slipped into another room with my phone and began texting my contacts back in San Diego, saying I had been kidnapped and would be killed if they didn't receive $500 ransom.

Armando excused himself a few minutes later, saying he needed to go find the woman. A short while later, the boy demanded money. By now, I had given all my cash to Armando. The young man dressed and left, leaving me alone in the room.

At once, Armando was pounding at the door. I let him back in and he started yelling in Spanish about all the drugs that we had used and demanding payment. Standing there naked and spent, I tried to explain in a combination of English and broken Spanish that we had agreed on a price and that I didn't have any more cash. Armando picked up my clothes and threw them at me, ordering me to dress. I was confused and frightened. Then he was pushing me out the door and down the stairs of the hotel and up the street, into the door of one of the bars on Revolucion. He walked me up to an ATM demanding I withdraw money for him. He was deliberate and controlled, ice cold. He stood over me; I felt his breath hot on my neck as he instructed me to withdraw the money from each card in my wallet and hand it to him until the money was all gone. I did not know the PIN for one card and this enraged him. "Mentiroso!" he screamed, calling me a liar in Spanish. Then he pushed me back out onto the street and forced me back up to the room, slamming the door behind us. Armando was insane, out of his mind, pacing and storming around the room and yelling into the phone in shotgun Spanish.

Armando told me the figure I still owed. It was insane. Suddenly, the conversation changed from what I owed "him" to what I owed "them." And although he did not explain exactly who "they" were, the implication was clear. I had pissed off a cartel. Armando waved the phone inches from my face. He told me I had fucked up and that I was in danger. My blood ran cold. He said I needed to fix this. I explained that I would get paid in a week and that I could fix it then. He told me that I would be doing exactly that but in the meanwhile, I would be working for them to pay off my debt. Arrangements were already being made for me to do so, he said, holding up the phone once more.

He said we were to leave the hotel and await further instructions. I didn't dare argue, his temper was explosive. He ordered me back down the stairs and onto the street. We walked a few blocks away and turned down a quiet residential street into a neighborhood of low-slung slums. Stray dogs cruised the streets and steel bars lined the windows. The streets and alleyways were deserted.

We passed through a ramshackle iron gate and stepped into a quiet and unassuming one-room apartment with an uneven floor. A threadbare sofa sat against one wall, and a twin mattress lay covered by a worn, knitted blanket against the other. Armando invited me to make myself comfortable on the bed and rest. I had a long night ahead of me, he said with a sly smile.

He stepped through a beaded curtain and engaged in low, hushed conversation with two women. "Did the gringo bring a gift?" I overheard one ask in Spanish.

"The gringo IS the gift," Armando replied. The trio snickered and laughed heartily a few feet away.

Armando came back into the room. He was more relaxed now than in the hotel. He asked for my wallet. He returned my credit cards to their slots, but pulled out my driver's license and studied it closely. He made another call, and relayed my driver's license number and address to the voice on the other end. Then he took a photo of my license with his phone, and texted it to someone. Confused, I sat in silence, not daring to speak. There were a few more trips through the beaded curtain and more urgent conversation.

Finally, Armando returned to the room and explained the plan. A car was to be registered in my name in El Paso, then driven to Juarez that evening. Late that night, I was to drive another vehicle from Tijuana to Ciudad Juarez where I would pick up a package at a motel, transfer into the vehicle that was registered to me, then transport the package and some passengers across the border. From that point on, I would be based at the motel in Juarez, and make this trip nightly. I would do this until my debt had been satisfied, or until I was no longer useful. This was my new life. My head spun.

This was terrifying enough but I had information that they did not which sent a chill down my spine. I thought back to the conversation at the border less than 24 hours ago. I had not yet had a chance to reach out to my friend in the U.S. to ask him to rescind the missing person's report. As far as the Customs and Border Patrol was concerned, I was still an endangered missing person. I would be pulled aside for secondary screening at the border and surely be nailed with my vehicle full of drugs and illegal immigrants. This was suicide.

Now, I faced a new dilemma: do I share this information with Armando and risk further harm? Either way, I was fucked. Telling him labeled me a liability at worst, and made me look uncooperative at the very least. I was caught between a rock and a hard place. My heart sank. I laid there mulling over my terrifying secret for the better part of the afternoon, praying and debating what to do. I considered making the journey and begging for help at the border, but I didn't think the Customs officials would believe me. Just before sunset, I decided to come clean. I told Armando. He flew into a rage, storming in and out of the kitchen and hurling insults and curses in Spanish. Another flurry of back and forth phone calls began. I was terrified as I lay there praying for mercy as Armando disappeared into the kitchen for yet another conference with the two women.

When Armando returned, the trip to Juarez was still on, much to my surprise. I laid there in shock and dread. An hour went by. Armando stepped into the kitchen just a few feet from my head. There was an urgent and hurried conversation, then another phone call. Perhaps Armando did not realize the extent of my Spanish abilities. Perhaps he simply no longer cared. But I heard it all clearly. The itinerary was modified. The trip to Juarez would be one way.

For the briefest moment, I laughed inwardly at the irony. How many times had I overheard plans for my murder in psychosis? Yet I had sobered quickly hours ago when first faced with Armando's hair-trigger temper and excitability. Now, I became extraordinarily calm and deathly quiet with my face turned towards the wall, laying on the tiny bed, listening to the hushed conversation from the next room.

Suddenly, I was overcome by a flash of anger that shot through my body as I traded fear for white hot rage. I was suddenly deeply and profoundly offended. Who did this two-bit favela hood think he was? Fuck this, the dick wasn't that good.

I did not panic, but rather began to center myself and systematically organize my thoughts much the way I did the day Scott tried to set me up in Los Angeles. The house was tiny and I had a direct shot to the open door. From there, it was just mere feet to the front gate which I knew I could swing open and be down the alley and onto the main road in no time. From there, however, I would be lost in the depths of the sprawling city. Without a phone or money I would be defenseless and without resources, a sitting duck.

I was still contemplating my plan when the drawn and tired, old woman stepped into the room. Armando introduced her as his mother. She bore a plate of food. I thanked her, and took a few bites of rice and beans, then handed back the plate. She looked at the food still on the plate, then at Armando angrily, and said something under her breath. She shuffled back into the kitchen and I heard the plate slam against the countertop. Armando stormed in behind her and there was rapid-fire Spanish. "Not good enough for the king!" the old woman exclaimed.

At once, Armando was shoving me out the door and into the alley in front of the apartment. I was furious now with nothing to lose. "Don't you think I hear all you say?" I demanded loudly in Spanish, jabbing my finger roughly into his chest. An old man passing by stopped to regard the spectacle. Armando reared back with rage, as if to strike me, then turned on his heel and stormed up the street shouting obscenities and clenching his fists. I realized I had gone too far. Before he had a chance to turn back around to attack, I bolted and ran full-speed down the street, turning the corner onto the bustling main road.

I realized with horror that I had left my backpack containing my passport and house keys behind but there was no going back now. I had to run as fast and as far as I could. I pushed through the swarming crowds of cosmopolitan Avenida Benito Juarez, past the neon pharmacias and the fragrant restaurants, and swerved down side streets past smoky food stalls and grizzled and jaded street vendors who barely raised an eyebrow as I stumbled past. To my surprise, Armando did not follow, or I was fast enough to lose him. Only safely many blocks away did I turn to look. I had shaken him free.

I had walked for about two hours when I realized I was completely and utterly lost in this sprawling city that stretched forever. Street names had become progressively unfamiliar, and the city was becoming more and more residential. I could no longer see the arch, my guiding landmark. I came across a main boulevard and spotted an Internet cafe ahead. For only 15 pesos, less than a dollar, I could connect to someone in the States and plead for help. I began begging on the street, accosting strangers and asking for 15 pesos, but no one would help me. I became increasingly more desperate and despondent and soon began to cry, which only served to frighten away the people I approached. Eventually, I gave up in utter despair and walked around the corner to a flight of steps that led down a long hill, and laid down upon them and began to sob.

CHAPTER 18

"Hello? Are you alright? Hello?" the young man was asking in English, crouched down before me and looking into my eyes with concern. He was attractive and well-dressed, as if commuting home from an office. It was as if an angel had alighted before me and I sat up and wiped my tears and tried to catch my breath. Between sobs, I explained that I was lost. He asked me where I lived. He said he had never heard of Maclovio Rojas. I told him I had lost all my money and my passport and my phone and didn't know what to do. He said his name was Hector and he didn't have any money either but he would help me get home. I started crying again and he grew uncomfortable.

Hector walked to the top of the stairs and asked some people on the street how to get to Maclovio Rojas. When he returned, he said we would have to take the Colectivo. He took me by the hand, helped me up, and we began walking in the direction of some battered, orange vans parked at the curb ahead and soon, we were in the back of a Colectivo and headed out of town.

The van stopped every few minutes to discharge or pick up other passengers and soon there were so many people packed into the rickety van that they were standing between the rows of seats. Hector explained in a low whisper that we were going to have to make a run for it when the van stopped on the side of the road near the main road into Maclovio Rojas. When the driver pulled over, I swung the door open and stepped out. Hector follow closely behind. Then he looked at me, smiled slyly, and said, "Run!" We set off of running up the dirt road as the driver leaned out the window yelling and cursing before pulling back onto the highway. I fell against Hector, laughing and gasping for breath, and realized I was starting to really like the mysterious knight in shining armor with the pirate smile who had rescued me from the streets of Tijuana.

Once inside, Hector showered while I made us a meal. Over dinner, we got to know one another. Hector was 22 and the son of a seamstress and a shopkeeper. His father died when Hector was a boy. His mother remarried, to a cruel and violent alcoholic who abused both Hector and his mother. Now, Hector had just lost his mother to cancer. He was mourning. He pulled a photo from his pocket of himself as a little boy seated on his mother's lap. The stepfather had thrown Hector out of the family home when his mother died. Hector was homeless, supporting himself by doing occasional construction work.

Until now, I wasn't sure if Hector was just a really nice guy or if he had something more in mind. As the evening wore on, he made it clear that his interests extended into the bedroom as well. We spent a passionate evening making languid love beneath the stars in the little house on the hill.

In the morning, Hector was forlorn. He said talking about his mother had made him sad. He wanted to get high so he could forget about his pain. He asked if I had any drugs. I was disappointed. I had enjoyed being sober with him in bed. I told him I didn't nor did I know where to get anything in town. He said he was sure he could find something. I said I needed to stay sober because I needed to figure out how to get back to work and I reminded him that we had no money. He grew restless and anxious, pacing around the house.

"Then we sell something," he said definitively and told me he had seen a pawnshop as we walked up the road to the house. Appraising my belongings, he settled on my laptop and a box fan. Knowing I needed money to get to work, I really couldn't argue. Besides, I told myself, I would make it back in tips in my first couple of shifts, so while I didn't much care for the idea, I knew it wasn't really that risky.

We headed down the road to the pawnshop where Hector did the deal and handed me the claim check and just enough money to get to work and back in the morning. He held on to the rest of the money himself. On the way out of the pawnshop, Hector chatted up a man on the side of the road and before I knew what was happening, he had a fistful of meth and a pipe, and we were back in the house in bed, high as hell.

In between rounds of lovemaking, Hector painted a picture of our future together. We would live in the little blue house on the hill. He would protect me and show me his Mexico. He was going to start his own construction firm with a crew of men working for him and he would come home to me each night. I was quickly falling for this rugged and masculine Latin lover and promptly forgot about work in the morning. By the time the drugs started to run thin around 2 a.m., I was falling in love.

Hector asked if he could wear my clothes. He said it made him feel closer to me. I told him to pick out an outfit. He stood in the center of my bedroom in form-fitting Calvin Klein jeans, a charcoal gray dress shirt, and a pair of lace-up dress shoes. He was gorgeous. He walked over to the nightstand and picked up my spare cell phone and took a selfie in the full length mirror. I couldn't have been prouder of the beautiful man in my presence. "I've got more shit in the other room for us baby, I'll go get it," he said and bent down to kiss my forehead, then walked out of the room turning out the light as he went.

I took a deep stretch and rolled over, feeling like the luckiest man in the world.

The front door slammed. In the aching and profound stillness that followed, stray dogs barked in the distance as Hector made his way back down the hill toward the village. As I laid there frozen still in the inky darkness of the predawn, shock and disbelief gave way to a deep and crushing sadness and ultimately, suffocating shame.

As the sun's first rays peeked over the hill, I rose from the bed and passed through the doorway and into the front room where my eyes lay sight of my empty wallet upside-down on the floor. My heart lurched and I let out a sob as the room spun and my heart shattered into a thousand pieces.

Heartbroken, abandoned, and destitute, I sat on the sofa collecting my thoughts. I was now stranded in a foreign country with no money, no phone, no passport, and no way of calling for help. I was deeply ashamed and emotionally overwrought, coming down from a lethal combination of methamphetamine and infatuation.

How had everything gone so wrong? I considered for a moment longer. This was truly beyond repair. I stood up and looked around the beautiful blue living room. It was so inviting and warm. I walked back into the bedroom and over to the window. I pulled open the metal shutters. Outside, the sun was high and the day was crisp and clean. Birdsong filled the air and music traveled on the light breeze. I took in a deep breath of fresh air. It was a picture perfect morning. Yet I could not connect with its idyllic beauty. I felt cold and lifeless.

I closed the squeaky metal shutters back again and latched them tightly. I climbed up onto my high bed and curled up. Above my head, the graceful pepper tree I so loved swayed gently, caressed by the sweet warm breeze. The scene was so peaceful and pastoral and yet I felt nothing but crushing, consuming sorrow. A single tear fell from my eye. I felt only a weight in my chest where my heart had been. I could barely breathe. Soon my body was racked with sobs. I laid there for some time regarding the rolling rack of clothing from which Hector had so gingerly selected his parting outfit a few hours prior. My eye was drawn to a pair of work pants on a hanger and the nylon belt resting through the loops.

I asked God for his forgiveness and then against great weight, I staggered from the bed and across the room. I pulled the belt from the pants. I hung the belt over the chrome rack and fashioned a noose. I slipped my head through it. With tear-filled eyes, I dropped towards my knees as the belt tightened around my neck. I felt the pounding pressure against the back of my eyes as I began to suffocate. The roar became deafening as I hung suspended for a moment or two, before in a rush of panic, I clawed wildly at the belt now digging into the side of my neck. I began scraping at the floor with my feet trying to stand and momentarily, I forced a finger between my neck and the belt. I gasped for breath. I ripped the belt from my neck and fell to the floor, wheezing and panting, praying for forgiveness.

I had been unbearably humiliated and degraded. The shame was suffocating. I could go no further down. I had hit rock bottom. I got on my knees in my bedroom and I prayed. I prayed for forgiveness then I asked God for strength and direction. "What do you want me to do?" I asked God aloud. Then I laid down on my bed perfectly still with my eyes closed and listened. I listened to the wind rustling the leaves of the peppertree above my window and the Volaris jets on approach overhead and the dogs barking in the distance, and I heard life going on despite my pain. And I knew I had to go on as well.

I had to get out into the fresh air and the sunshine. I walked to the dresser, pulled out a pair of shorts, and slipped them on. There was something in the pocket. I reached in and to my surprise pulled out two 20 peso bills. My heart leapt. I had my answer loud and clear.

I always used Uber in Mexico. But I knew the Colectivo to Refugio, the next town over, was 17 pesos. I did not know what the fare from Refugio to the border was, but if it was more than 17 pesos, I could always turn around and come back to the house. If I did have enough to get to the border, I could get to the Cricket store and use my one remaining credit card to buy another phone, then download the San Diego Transit Authority app and charge a bus ride. I could ride to SeaWorld where I kept a uniform in my locker. I could explain to my managers what had happened and ask them to let me wait some tables for tips. Once I had some cash in my pocket, I would be okay. I could begin again. It was risky. I only had one shot. Aside from the one ride with Hector at my side, I had never used the Colectivo. The idea terrified me.

The main highway in front of Maclovio Rojas was busy and hectic, filled with fast-moving traffic and lumbering semi-trucks. The Colectivo vans zoomed by quickly with only a general direction scribbled on the windshield in marker or soap and I did not know the city well enough to know which van to flag down. I did know, however, that if I could get to Refugio, the vans would be staged in the parking lot of the Bodega Aurrura supermarket for the onward journey. There I could ask someone which one to board before just jumping in. This would require bravery like I'd never shown before. I had no phone and no passport and no margin for error whatsoever. One false move and I could be lost deep at the mercy of the teeming and unfamiliar city, lost forever with no recourse. My heart was in my throat as I walked terrified back down the road and headed toward the main highway.

Several vans passed while I tried to make sense of the barely visible destinations written on the windshields. I couldn't understand any of it. None of the destinations sounded familiar. Riders gathered around and flagged down their vans, climbed inside, and pulled away leaving me baffled and embarrassed alone on the side of the road, frustrated to the point of tears.

I couldn't take the embarrassment any longer. I flagged down the next passing van and asked the driver, "Refugio?" He answered in the affirmative so I climbed aboard. As we neared the familiar green and yellow supermarket I yelled out self-consciously, "Aqui, por favor!" and the driver pulled to a stop on the roadside. I handed over my 20 peso note and he returned 3 pesos change. Success.

As expected, there were several vans idling in the parking lot and it was easy to determine which one was headed to San Ysidro. Much to my relief, the fare was 19 pesos. I said a silent prayer of thanks and climbed aboard.

Half an hour later, I alighted at the border and passed through Customs and Border Patrol.

The sense of relief and accomplishment I felt brought tears to my eyes. I marveled at the resilience and inner strength that had brought me from nearly ending my life to divining my way across a crowded foreign city on faith and a pocket full of pesos. I thanked Armando and Hector for helping me see just what I was really made of.

By the time I reached San Diego, I had missed my shift at

SeaWorld. I stood downtown at the corner of Broadway and Park. I was safe, but I was tired. I had run as far as I could and I was out of strength. Only a few hours earlier I had tried to end my life in my beautiful blue home on the hill. Now penniless, I could not return if I wanted to. I looked up to the sky and I surrendered. Suddenly, I began to cry as the fatigue and stress of the day overwhelmed me. I looked around, embarrassed. No one noticed me standing in tears on the busy corner.

There is a weathered Victorian on a tree-lined street in the East Village neighborhood of San Diego. The crisis house is a soft place to land when life has become too much to bear. A safe house where one finds help to pick the pieces back up and start anew. Instinctively, I began walking in that direction. I was crying and shaking as I stood on the porch. I wanted so badly to run, but something deep within told me to knock on the door. A therapist answered the door. I looked into his eyes, so compassionate and understanding, and all I could do was sob. I knew I was home at last. We sat together on the rickety old porch as the sun set and watched the city pass by as I told my long and winding story from the very beginning. For the first time in years, I realized I had a fighting chance at health and happiness. And that night, I fell fast asleep in America's Finest City.

www.ingramcontent.com/pod-product-compliance
Lightning Source LLC
LaVergne TN
LVHW091251080426
835510LV00007B/217